ALSO BY DEBORAH JOHNSON

BOOKS
Stuck is Not a Four-Letter Word
Walking with the Hymns: A Devotional Guide
My Father's Favorite Hymns: A Piano-Vocal Music Book

MUSICALS
Tsarina: Book, Music and Lyrics
Stiltz: Music and Lyrics
One Little Kiss: Book, Music and Lyrics

MUSIC ALBUMS
Wayfarer's Journey
The Hero Inside
My Father's Favorite Hymns
Office #7 (Stiltz the Musical)
Double Grandé Experience: Broadway to Hollywood
(with Wayland Pickard)
Classics Rock (Double Grandé with Wayland Pickard)
Tsarina the Musical
Chocolate Songs of Love
One Little Kiss the Musical
Musical Moments
Merry Christmas Too
Classical Spice
Destiny

Many selections of Sheet Music on SheetMusicPlus.com

Music for Kids

When to Start Piano Lessons

Bonus Chapters:

Music and Stress
What about the Mozart Effect?

DEBORAH JOHNSON

 DJWorksMusic.com

MUSIC FOR KIDS
When to Start Piano Lessons

Copyright ©2015 Deborah Johnson

Johnson, Deborah, author

Issued in print and electronic format
ISBN 978-0-9885879-3-9

Characters in this book are fictional. Names, characters, places and incidents
are products of the author's imagination or are used facetiously.

Cover art by Vikiana, ©Deborah Johnson
Drawings by Benjamin, ©Deborah Johnson
Back cover photo by Jessica Johnson

Visit Deborah's website at DJWorksMusic.com
DJWorksMusic.com/music-for-kids/

This book is dedicated to all those musicians who are working so hard to make
a difference. Many could be making a lot more money in other fields, but they
chose to make a difference with their art and the joy they give others from
creating the music they have in their soul.

Contents

KUDOS and REVIEWS ix
ACKNOWLEGEMENTS xi

INTRODUCTION: When to Start Piano Lessons xii
  Why this book? xii
  Should your child have talent to start music lessons? xiv

CHAPTER ONE: The Importance of Music Lessons 1
  When to first ask about music lessons 1
  Benefits of music as a part of your child's education 2
  Music in the schools 4
  Music with a private teacher 5
  What age should your child start lessons? 6
  Benefit of community music classes 7
  Types of classes: Kodaly, Orff and others 8
  Take-away principles 10

CHAPTER TWO: Differences between Pianos and Keyboards 15
  What type of piano or keyboard should you get and why? 16
  Differences between acoustic and electronic pianos 17
  Electronic synthesizer keyboards 18
  Acoustic pianos 18
  Benefits of each type of piano and keyboard 20
  Why start your child on piano and not another instrument? 20
  Take-away principles 22

CHAPTER THREE: Searching for a Piano and a Private Teacher   24
    What to look for in a piano   25
    What to look for in a teacher   26
    Take-away principles   29

CHAPTER FOUR: Hiring the Right Teacher   31
    Referrals and professional organizations   32
    What type of things should the private teacher teach?   33
    Are online piano programs good for beginners?   34
    Take-away principles   36

CHAPTER FIVE: Learning the Basics: Notes, Chords   39
    Learning the basic notes   40
    Learning the basic five-note scales   41
    Learning the basic chords   42
    Having good posture   44
    Take-away principles   46

CHAPTER SIX: Learning the Basics: Arpeggios, Pedal   48
    What are arpeggios and why play them?   51
    Using the pedal correctly   51
    Take-away principles   55

CHAPTER SEVEN: Learning the Basics: Improvisation   58
    What is basic Improvisation?   59
    Can a beginning student learn to improvise?   61
    Take-away principles   63

CHAPTER EIGHT: Learning the Basics: Hand Position   65
    Relaxing the hands, arms and shoulders   66
    How to work on relaxation while playing the piano   68
    Take-away principles   69

CHAPTER NINE: Learning the Basics: Performance 71
How to cope with nervousness 73
How to implement perfect practice and concentration 75
The importance of memorization 76
Take-away principles 77

CHAPTER TEN: Setting Goals and Deadlines 80
Setting new goals for the beginner 81
Take-away principles 84

CHAPTER ELEVEN: Music and Stress 85
The calming and relaxing power of music 86
How music can affect the heart rate 86
How music can affect brain function 88
Using music as a diversion 88
Using music in therapy 89
Benefits of studying a musical instrument 91
Take-away principles 93

CHAPTER TWELVE: The Mozart Effect 94
Why Albert Einstein played Mozart 94
What is the Mozart Effect? 95
Mozart and spatial reasoning 95
Why the music of Mozart? 96
The commercial power of the Mozart Effect 97
Playing Mozart and playing football 97
Should you play Mozart for your babies in the womb? 99
Does playing classical music really make your kids smarter? 100
Take-away principles 102

QUOTABLE MUSICIAN QUOTES 103
DEFINITIONS OF MUSICAL TERMS 106
ABOUT DEBORAH 109

KUDOS and REVIEWS

Music education is an important and worthwhile endeavor for any family, but most people don't know where or how to begin. I heartily endorse this book, which is the only one I've ever seen that succinctly and directly addresses many of the questions and concerns I frequently hear from parents who are interested in starting their children in their musical journey. The information that Deborah provides will undoubtedly guide parents in building a successful foundation in music for their family, and help curb the high drop out rate in music education. Highly recommended for anyone that wants to get their children started with a positive approach to music creation as part of their lifestyle, benefiting them holistically for their lifetime.

-LAURA SULLIVAN
Grammy Award® Winning Composer & Recording Artist
Compositions featured in film & T.V.
B.A. Music, M.A. Psychology[1]

---

1. http://www.laura-sullivan.com

In her book, Deborah addresses the overwhelming questions new parents may ask, and even the questions they may never have thought to ask or research. She shows the great impact that music can have from early disciplines in children, all the way to the affects of music in managing stress later in life. I have seen first hand the challenges in getting a child to start and progress into a well-seasoned musician, as well as the huge benefits music can have in adult lives. Deborah gives parents help in understanding what it takes to help their children to be successful, and great insight and guidelines as they consider starting this journey with their children.

-SANDY MACKINGA
Voice and Violin Instructor for 40 years; Member M.T.A. for 25 years
Music Director, Bay Cities Community Church[1]

I can't overstate the value of music education, and not just for those who seem to have talent or special interest in music. Music touches the soul, like very few other things can in this universe. Why is music so important, specifically piano? Deborah answers those questions and more in her book. As music programs are declining in numbers and support, the responsibility comes back to parents and caregivers in the home, which is actually the way it used to be. Music for Kids is a must-read for answering some of the basic questions, asked over and over on how, when and why. Deborah is an absolute pro, whom I had the chance of working with some years ago. She was one of the few pianists who could follow all my multiple key changes on the organ!

-GENE ROBERSON
Concert Organist & Pianist; Roland Atelier Organ Artist
Composer; Church Music Director
Instructor and organ dealer[2]

---

1. Hear Sandy Mackinga playing the violin on the album Wayfarer's Journey. http://DJWorksMusic.com/wayfarers-journey/
2. http://generoberson.com

ACKOWLEDGEMENTS

Thank you to those teachers who have helped to engrain and fuel a deep love of music in my life. Yes, I could have gone into another field as law or business, but I chose music early on. I was told I had a natural talent, but still needed to study and work hard to develop that talent. I have also found that it is important to know the basic legal and business principles to stay working in my chosen profession of music.

I am deeply grateful for my husband Greg who has the understanding of my passion and gifts. He has listened patiently for years to new compositions and ideas, and has read numerous articles and book chapters. He asks the "why" behind any firm statement I make. I love our times talking through ideas on our patio and appreciate his listening ear, especially after I've had one too many cups of caffeinated coffee! Having someone like him in my life is a true gift.

A special thank you also to Sandra Grajeda, who read and edited this book. Her chosen profession was law, but she has a deep love of music. She has given so much of herself not only in editing this project, but also other projects as well as served as stage manager for the world premiere of two of my musicals. That was truly a labor of love and I will always appreciate her gifts of time and attention to detail.

INTRODUCTION

Music for Kids: When to Start Piano Lessons

Why this book?

I was recently at my local market when I ran into an acquaintance. She excitedly started telling me about her granddaughter's recent performance and couldn't get over how good her granddaughter was, elaborating about her stage presence and voice. Then she came to the question I've been asked thousands of times, "When is a good age to start her in voice lessons?" Knowing her granddaughter was about six years old, I realized tens of thousands of mothers, grandmothers and caregivers are asking this same question. I was not planning on writing a book on *Music for Kids*; it was not in my yearly or even multi-yearly plans to do so and was one of the farthest things from my mind. However, I was finding a whole new generation was asking the same question that grandmother asked me without a current place to find answers. That propelled me to write this book.

To illustrate the anxiety and confusion involved in this decision, when I mentioned this book to a group of colleagues, many whom were *Grammy Nominees* and *Grammy Award Winners*, I began to receive varying opinions based on their own stories. Some had started studying music at a very young age, however, there were several that had started much older, as in high school, still with much success. Interestingly the common thread in their stories was how thankful they were in learning essential piano and the importance of taking private lessons.

If at all possible, I believe music should be a part of every child's education and specifically include some sort of piano or keyboard instruction. This doesn't mean that all children need to take private lessons, as it is a luxury that many cannot afford. However, many can afford some sort of training for their children. How to spend extra resources, whether on music, on sports or on other areas, is somewhat daunting at times. What about private lessons? Are they even worth pursuing for your child? I found the key to my professional colleague's success was a deep desire to learn coupled with private lessons. That was also my personal experience.

What about online learning programs? Will your child really learn and be disciplined enough with one of those programs? I will answer those questions and more. Hopefully what is included in this book will help you with your decisions and even increase your commitment to music education.

Besides answering the question of if and when to start your child in private lessons, I have included two bonus chapters. The first deals with how music can *help relieve stress*. This is an interesting and informative chapter for adults and even college students to read. The second deals with the *Mozart Effect*. There has been much research and many varying opinions on the *Mozart Effect* and the question of whether classical music can truly make your kids smarter. I address these questions with some realistic facts and opinions that may help you make your own decision on that theory.

My current profession is not primarily focused on teaching, though I started teaching privately, even adults, at the age of thirteen. I obtained both my secondary teaching credential and Masters Degree and I have taught every level through graduate school. I have pursued teaching private students, speaking and leading workshops and master classes more than classroom instruction. For a number of years, my main work has been as a composer, recording artist, and professional pianist and vocalist. I have performed for many private events and organizations such as Disney and others, as well as for headliner concerts around the U.S. and abroad. I love what I do and I love music. I believe in the power of music and hope to instill a commitment to include it in every child's education—especially learning the piano or basic keyboard, which provides a solid foundation for lifelong learning and enjoyment.

Should your child have talent to start music lessons?

This is a question many young parents ask. Should you only start your child in music lessons if you feel they have true talent? How important are private music lessons and are they really worth the money and effort? What other options are there for getting your child interested and involved in music at a young age? I will be addressing the whole subject of *Music for Kids* and answering many of these questions by dropping in on the discussion of two fictional friends, Katie and Rachel.

I believe every child has creative potential and that music should be added to their overall education. Dr. T. Berry Brazelton, Dr. Bruce Perry and other child development experts list music as one of the ten things every child needs for the best start in life (*Ten Things Every Child Needs for the Best Start in Life!*)[1] Some children will be more exuberant than others, but

---

1. Dr. T. Berry Brazelton, "Ten Things Every Child Needs for the Best Start in Life!" Consumervision DVD, October 5, 2004.

I believe most every child has the ability to learn some of the basic principles of music and it takes a strong commitment from the parents and/or caregivers to encourage practice and consistency. This book focuses on piano and keyboard, as I believe piano is the best instrument for learning the basics, whether or not the child is also studying another instrument. At the end of each chapter are some take-away principles that will summarize and give additional details for the subjects that Katie and Rachel discuss in their dialogue.

Katie and Rachel are good friends who met in college and are both now raising young children. Rachel's kids, Catherine and Eric, are nine and eleven, respectively. Katie's daughter, Shannon is seven. They don't see each other very often, but as their paths start to coincide again, they quickly start communicating about music lessons and the details involved in providing lessons for their children. Let's follow their journey and stop in to hear their conversations.

Katie watches Shannon, her daughter, as she performs on stage. Shannon is beaming and Katie immediately starts wondering if her daughter has a future in music and show business.

CHAPTER ONE

The Importance of Music Lessons

Every child should have the opportunity to learn the basics of music, preferably on a piano or keyboard. –Deborah Johnson

When to first ask about music lessons

Katie can't believe her eyes. She is watching her daughter Shannon in her first full school performance and Shannon is absolutely stealing the show. She has never seen Shannon light up like she does now, in front of an audience. Katie is trying to suppress her giggles of delight in what she sees and immediately starts wondering if her daughter has a future in music and show business. Of course, Shannon has only just turned seven years old, but Katie wants to give her daughter the very best she can give her.

Katie remembers back to the day Shannon was born and the miracle it was to even be able to have a child after several miscarriages. She remembers holding her little baby girl in her arms, swaddled in a small blanket and her mind then leaps to today, seven years later. Time has flown faster than she imagined and even though her job keeps her fairly busy, she doesn't want to miss a single one of Shannon's activities. Katie decides right

1

then and there she wants to fuel Shannon's interest in music, yet not push her too hard to make her disinterested, as she was growing up, and fast.

The performance suddenly ends and Katie jumps to her feet with applause, joined by the rest of the audience, including parents, grandparents and a few siblings. After the teacher gathers the performers together, looking like a group of jackrabbits jumping and wiggling, they take their bows. Shannon then runs to her mom, flush with excitement. "Did you see me, mom? Did you...did you see me?"

"Of course I saw you Shannon! You were wonderful! You stole the show!"

"I didn't steal anything mom, I promise!"

"No, Shannon, it's only an expression! You were terrific!"

Seeing her best friend, Shannon suddenly jumps up again and starts running off, "Can I go to Susie's, just for a while?"

Katie calls after her, "Only for about an hour, then I'll pick you up," but Shannon has already run across the room, too far away to hear her.

Katie smiles, making a mental note that she will look into private lessons for Shannon right away. She also decides she deserves a mocha chip Frappuccino for being such a good mom, one of her Starbucks favorites.

Benefits of music as a part of your child's education

As Katie walks into her local Starbucks, she sees Rachel. Since their kids are in different grades at school, their schedules don't often coincide.

Katie quickly stands by Rachel in line, "Rachel! Good to see you!"

Rachel, "Hi Katie! What has it been, a couple months?"

"At least. I'm so glad I ran into you today because I have a question I think you can help me with!"

"About?"

"I think Shannon has some real musical talent. Actually I think she has that 'it star quality.' You went through this with your kids didn't you?"

"Deciding whether or not they have real talent?'"

"Well no, of course they do!" laughs Katie

"Oh yes, our genius kids!"

"Uh...genius...mmm...I'm not so sure about that one!" Katie and Rachel move forward in line, "But yes, all our kids have some talent!"

"Just look at their parents!"

Katie pauses, "Questionable! But I do remember that we all played classical music while pregnant."

Rachel, nodding, "Playing Mozart was supposed to make our kids smarter."

"I'm not totally sure how that worked."

"It sure made us feel better. The music was calming and I even played classical music while studying for my college exams."

"Did it help?"

"I passed!"

"Now I know you're even more qualified to answer my question!"

"I'll definitely give it my best shot! "

Music in the schools

"I just saw Shannon in her school play production and she just loves being on stage! She comes alive when she's in front of an audience; I couldn't take my eyes off of her!" Katie almost jumps with excitement, "She ended up stealing the show!"

"I know what you mean! Sometimes I feel the same way about Eric and Catherine when they're in a production."

"So you get it. What should I do? Should I get her in some sort of music performance group or singing lessons? I have heard it's good to start giving them lessons very young, and I'm afraid I might have waited too long. Shannon's growing up so fast."

"It's good you're thinking about this as so many programs have been cut in the schools. They also don't have time or the resources to spend any more as there are so many other subjects they need to cover. Have you thought about piano lessons?"

"My experience with piano lessons wasn't so positive growing up. I hated to practice and the music was boring. I'm afraid Shannon would end up hating piano like I did."

"You can't really hate piano."

"Actually, it was just the lessons."

"It was probably just the teacher."

"Right, but Shannon just loves to sing and perform."

"The piano will really help Shannon's ear in her singing. When you learn a language, you learn the vowels, the combination of those vowels; then words and sentences, and how to read those sentences. In the same way, piano helps you learn the basics of the language and the sound of music."

"Wow!" Katie pauses, then responds, "Ideally I'd love for music to be a big part of her life and education, right along with her schoolwork, but what if she's bored like I was?"

They now both arrive at the front of the Starbucks line and Rachel orders her latté with a double shot of espresso, then she continues, "Piano lessons don't have to be boring."

Music with a private teacher

"So are both Eric and Catherine taking piano lessons?"

"Yes, I have them both in private lessons."

"That has to be expensive!" Katie then orders her mocha chip Frappuccino. "You have two—I shouldn't complain."

"It's not really as expensive as you may think. Plus, their teacher gave me a good deal with both of them. I treat music lessons as a part of their education. Just look how much it costs to be in sports programs!"

"I know! I'm just starting to see that. Some of those traveling teams...."

"Ridiculous!"

Katie laughs, "I just figure I'll never be able to quit my job!"

"Same here! And if Rick ever misses a child support payment, I'm really sunk!"

What age should your child start lessons?

"You work so hard. Shannon doesn't seem too interested in dance or sports right now, but I am interested in getting her into some sort of music program. When should I look for a piano teacher and where should I look?"

"How old is Shannon now?"

"She just turned seven."

"That's right, she's a couple years younger than my kids. I wouldn't start Shannon in private lessons at least until she turns eight."

"But isn't that a little too late, and won't she lose interest by then? I don't want her to lose this excitement."

"She shouldn't, especially if you enroll her in some other classes."

"Like what?"

Benefit of community music classes

"If I were you, I'd look into some of the group community classes with rhythm and movement. Those type of classes keep young children involved in music, but it's not as focused and demanding as the private lessons."

"But I started piano lessons at age five. Isn't earlier better?"

"Well look what happened—you quit! Could you even sit still for twenty minutes at five years old?"

Katie, "Probably not!"

"My point exactly. Your poor teacher probably had to coax you to sit still even for a couple minutes at a time, and just think; you're a girl. Do you know what most little boys are like at five or seven? Many kids, but not all—don't get me wrong here—many who start private lessons that young burn out by the age of ten. Generally, they aren't ready for the type of structure and discipline that private lessons require at such a young age."

"I do see your point."

"A group community class that includes movement, simple rhythm instruments and singing keeps younger children interested and growing. It also adds to their basic ability to feel the music."

Types of classes: Kodaly, Orff and others

"I can see why they'd do well, moving all the time—just like the school program Shannon was just in!"

"Exactly! But many of those classes usually add more music and rhythm too; and they still have some sort of simple program at the end."

"Shannon would probably really enjoy that. I just got the city paper with all the community classes listed on it yesterday."

"Some of the community classes will incorporate some of the Kodaly method and Orff instruments too."

"What are those?"

"Don't worry too much about the terminology; it's mostly in the teacher training. From what I understand, the Kodaly method incorporates songs they know, like folk songs, and Orff adds simple rhythm instruments. Most community classes have a very good, enthusiastic teacher who may be trained in college to use some of those methods. Some of the teachers also have a music studio of their own."

"How did you find all this out?"

"Mainly by trial and error, believe me!"

"Are there singing classes?"

"Maybe, but there's usually always singing involved in most classes. You can definitely ask!"

"Then I might want to take a class too!"

"I don't think they'll let you! But definitely sit in at least once in awhile. Some parents just drop off their kids." Rachel's latté is ready and she grabs it. "I've got to run. Work scheduled an extra meeting."

"Is that the reason for a double shot of espresso this late in the day?"

"That, and I just got a promotion. With all of the additional training I have to do, my plate is very full."

"Time for a work diet! Don't stress out too much!"

"Too late! But really, let me know what classes you find for Shannon!"

Katie, now picking up her Frappuccino, "I will! Thanks so much for the great advice."

Rachel runs out and Katie takes a sip of her Frappuccino. Katie is so excited about looking up a class for Shannon that she almost forgets to pick Shannon up at Susie's. However, a call from her husband, who is going to arrive home late, reminds her to swing by her daughter's best friend's house. She decides to make dinner easy tonight and stop for take-out on their way home.

❖❖❖ TAKE-AWAY PRINCIPLES

1. What age should a child start private lessons?
Piano lessons are a perfect supplement to an education. In my opinion, incorporating the music lesson and practice right along with the child's schoolwork and homework is optimal. Some elementary school districts still have music in their curriculum, but I'm a strong believer in the addition of private instruction if possible. It is best to begin with private lessons at the age of eight to nine for girls and more like the age of nine for boys.

2. Is there something you can enroll your child in before starting private lessons?
Community group classes are perfect to keep children interested in music and will increase their ability and learning in rhythm and movement. Even a dance or gymnastic class with a lot of movement and music will captivate very young children and help with their development of rhythmic feel.

3. What if there are no community classes in your area?
If there are no community classes or programs in your area, look for something online. Many online programs also have video. Any online program will take an increased commitment of the parent or caregiver to be involved with their child. Another idea would be to get together with other families in your area with children of similar ages to do musical activities together.

4. What about taking singing lessons?
As most children's full lung capacity doesn't develop until at least 10, private vocal lessons should occur later, even middle school or high school. However, if singing is incorporated in the student's instrumental lessons, with the student singing along with the song melodies, scales and songs, it will develop the student's ear and musicality. Learning piano provides the basic foundation of the musical language for any student. If the child

10

is taking singing lessons at a young age of eight to ten, I would insist on adding basic piano or keyboard training.

5. Should you invest in private lessons only if your child has extraordinary talent?
In my opinion, absolutely not. We do not enroll a child in a math class just because they have a special skill in math. The class is a place to be exposed to math and develop a new skill. The same principle holds true with music. As the student progresses in music education after some years, the decision can then be made whether or not to continue. There are many studies that confirm the benefit of adding music to a child's education.

6. So what are all those Kodaly method classes, Orff instruments and other programs all about?
I will summarize some of those programs below for your information. There are others, but these have been some of the main ones in the past decades. Many of their principles, music and theory infiltrate current classes and curriculums.

Kodaly: Developed by Zoltan Kodaly in the 1940's and came to North America in the late 1960's. This method teaches music through the child's native tongue, or songs of their culture learned at home (like folk songs). Kodaly believed music should be introduced at a very young age and first with the voice as the primary instrument.

Orff: Developed in the 1920s by German composer Carl Orff (1895-1982) and translated into many languages. This method uses the voice, movement, and playing various-sized drums, xylophones and chimes. The students physically experience the beat, meter, tempo and rhythm, expressing it through dance and instruments. Many colleges train teachers in this method.

Suzuki: Shinichi Suzuki, a violinist, educator and philosopher developed his method of teaching in Japan and began putting it to use shortly after World War II. The Suzuki method came to North America in the late 1960's and expanded to include methods for cello, piano and flute. Suzuki realized children could learn music through listening, imitation and repetition and based his method on teaching this way with love and dedication. He taught using the concept character first, ability second. His goal was to embrace the whole child nurturing the love of music and the development of a fine character rather than just the mastering of a musical instrument. Formal lessons begin as early as age three.[1]

Yamaha: A piano group lesson system was introduced into the school system in 1954. Genichi Kawakami, Yamaha's president, established the Yamaha Music Foundation to develop and promote music education nationally. The method assumes music is a language children can learn naturally in the same way they learn their spoken and written language: *we hear, we imitate, we speak and we read.*[2] The program is age-specific with classes taught to a group of students (typically 8 to 10 per class). Courses are for children from age two to primary grades. They also have a grade examination system that more than 9.5 million people have been involved in over the last 40 years.

Music Teacher's Association (MTA): In 1876 Theodore Presser and his colleagues founded the Music Teachers National Association with the purpose of advancing the value of music study and music making to society while supporting the careers and professionalism of teachers of music. Presently, there are nearly 22,000 members in 50 states and more than 500 local

1. http://www.suzukimusic.org.au/suzuki.htm
2. http://ymsboston.com/-/music-lesson-methodology/

affiliates. They have a Professional Certification Program and some states include a Certificate of Merit program.

National Association for Music Education (NAfME): Founded in 1907 and is among the world's largest arts education organizations. It is the only association that focuses on all aspects of music education. It advocates for teachers and students with elected officials. NAfME's activities and resources have been largely responsible for the establishment of music education as a profession, for the promotion and guidance of music study as an integral part of the school curriculum, and for the development of the National Standards for Arts Education. Originally called Music Supervisors' National Conference, then in 1934, Music Educators National Conference (MENC), then in 2011, National Association for Music Education.[1]

1. http://www.nafme.org/about/

There are different types of keyboards and acoustic pianos.
For acoustics, there are grand pianos and upright pianos of
different sizes. There are many types of electronic keyboard
synthesizers, also of different sizes. Some electronic
instruments are weighted and some, un-weighted.

CHAPTER TWO

Differences between Pianos and Keyboards

Learning the fundamentals of music on a piano provides a crucial understanding of music theory and development of hand-eye coordination. –Deborah Johnson

After talking with Rachel, Katie could hardly wait to get Shannon enrolled in a community music class. She found a class that looked perfect, but it didn't start for another month in the middle of summer. However, the class would last eight weeks with a performance at the end so she felt it would be worth the wait. Shannon continued to sing around the house and when Katie told Shannon about the upcoming class she had signed her up for, Shannon started asking her about it every day.

Katie was glad Shannon was so excited about the class, but was relieved when it finally started, as she was tired of Shannon asking about it so much. When the class began, Katie sat all the way through the first session, as she knew she wouldn't be able to stay through every session after that. However, she did catch enough of the classes to see Shannon was having fun and also saw some of the things she would be learning about rhythm and movement. The eight weeks went by quickly and when it came time for the small performance at the end, Katie knew the class was a good choice, at least for the present time.

Before the first class even ended, Katie enrolled Shannon in another session that lasted twelve weeks. This next class included more movement along with the students playing some rhythm instruments, keeping time with the music. Katie could tell Shannon was growing in her ability, at least with an increased attention span and ability to keep time with the musical beat. Katie decided she'd enroll Shannon in one more class before looking into private piano lessons soon after she turned eight, but first she had some questions about pianos. She didn't have a piano and didn't know if she could even fit one in her house.

Katie decided she'd text Rachel with her questions, as she had not seen her since their last encounter at Starbucks nearly six months before. But first, she decided she deserved a treat, so she walked in the coffee shop and ordered a cinnamon dolce sugar-free latté. As luck would have it, when she stepped up to the counter, Rachel walked in the door.

What type of piano or keyboard should you get and why?

"Rachel! I was just thinking about you and was going to send you a text!" Katie finishes ordering her latté, then steps back in line with Rachel.

"Work has been pretty crazy and I've been gone a lot. There's so much out-of-town travel and I hardly have time to stop for coffee!"

"I haven't been back here much, either. You sound stressed."

"I still like my job, but they're just expecting too much for one person right now. I don't think it will last forever, though."

16

"I hope not. You really look tired."

"I am tired, that's for sure, but I'm really O.K. Tell me how are things going with Shannon. Did you get her into any music classes?"

"Great memory! You gave me such good advice; she loved her community classes! Now I'm thinking more seriously about private piano lessons, but we don't even have a piano. Actually, I'm not sure we have room for a piano."

Differences between acoustic and electronic pianos

"I was lucky that I inherited a piano from my grandmother. Some pianos and keyboards don't take much room."

"Pianos and Keyboards; it's confusing. There are so many different types and I don't want to spend a whole lot of money."

As Rachel gets to the front of the counter, she stops to order a sugar-free non-fat steamer, "Have you thought about a weighted synthesizer keyboard?"

"I'm not sure I understand what a weighted synthesizer keyboard is. I've heard about a synthesizer, a keyboard and all sorts of different pianos. With so many choices, what's the best way to go?"

"Well, you do know the difference between an acoustic and electronic piano, right?"

"They're like guitars as far as I know. One has a cable and one doesn't. But I've seen some of the acoustic grand pianos that also have plugs and cables. Why do you need to plug a grand piano in?"

"Some of them can play on their own, but we don't need to get into that quite yet."

"Sounds good to me."

Electronic synthesizer keyboards

"Let's start with the synthesizer keyboards. There's a weighted keyboard and an un-weighted keyboard."

"One's heavier than the other?"

"In a way, but there's more to it than that. Most acoustic piano keys are naturally weighted because they have little hammers inside that hit the strings when you press down on the keys."

"So you're talking about the actual weight of the piano keys."

"Basically. A weighted keyboard is stiffer to the touch. An un-weighted keyboard is usually easy to press, like an organ."

"And you're suggesting for me…?"

"For the piano student, I suggest a weighted instrument to build finger strength and to develop correct hand position."

Acoustic pianos

"That makes sense. I've seen the inside of a grand piano when they're being played and I've seen the movement." The barista calls Katie's name and she retrieves her latté. "What are the big differences between the acoustic pianos that are upright and the grand pianos with lids that raise? I'm assuming the upright pianos also have hammers?"

"Yes, they work exactly the same, but the uprights are usually not open to where you can see the hammers hit the strings. They can also fit in a more compact space against a wall, but if the back is open, the sound is projected toward the wall and not the room, different than grand pianos." Rachel makes a large circle with her hands for emphasis, "When the lid of a grand piano is open, the piano will fill a room with sound."

"Ah, like on most concert stages! Does the size of a grand piano make a big difference?"

"Somewhat. There are baby grands."

"So like babies, they're small?"

"Right, five feet."

"I'm afraid I don't even have room for one of those."

"Actually, acoustic pianos are becoming more rare these days with all the great electric piano options. I have a parlor grand, but only because it was my grandmother's."

"A parlor grand sounds like it belongs in a castle."

"It does, doesn't it? A parlor grand is six feet long."

"I love the look of those very large pianos you see on a stage. How big are they? "

"Usually nine feet."

"Wow."

"You'd need a big room and a lot of money."

"I'll pass!" laughs Katie.

Benefits of each type of piano and keyboard

"Even though I personally prefer an acoustic piano, you may want to seriously consider an electronic weighted keyboard. They don't cost as much and will fit in a smaller space." The barista calls Rachel's name and she picks up her steamer as she continues, "Electronic pianos also don't need to be tuned. An acoustic piano will have subtle differences for a discerning listener, plus the weight of the keys help a student build finger strength. But a good weighted electronic synthesizer keyboard should do much of the same thing."

"That sounds like what I need." Katie continues, "No double espresso today, huh?"

Sighing, "Not today—I'm adding more protein in my diet— nine grams in every eight ounces of milk!"

"Ooh—sounds good!"

"Even better, it's a 'non-fat' steamer."

"Definitely on my list now." Katie continues, "You know, I've not asked you your opinion on one more thing."

"Just one?" Katie laughs and Rachel continues, "I think we have time."

Why start your child on piano and not another instrument?

"Is piano really the best instrument to start Shannon on? I mean there are a lot of other instruments."

"Learning piano provides the framework to develop a deeper appreciation of music, whether an athlete or actor; a mechanic or poet. The piano provides such a great basic of learning the whole language of music, whether or not the student continues primarily on that instrument."

"Like learning to play with both hands together?"

"Yes, and learning the notes of both the treble and bass clef as well as the basic chords. A friend of mine was a music major in college and apparently you have to pass a piano proficiency class in order to graduate, no matter what instrument you play. Many of the instrumental and vocal majors had a hard time passing the test; and some of them even had a hard time in their basic music theory classes."

"I doubt if Shannon will get that far, but you never know!"

"Right you are. But it really shows the value of learning the piano, even for students learning other instruments and choosing music as a profession." Rachel smiles and takes her first sip, "Mmmm...love steamers! Back to keyboards, you can buy one new or used. There are usually many very good used weighted keyboards available online."

They both start leaving, "That's a great idea. Thanks so much Rachel. I'll start looking now."

"Let me know what you find and give me a call if you have any more questions!"

"Will do! Thanks again."

❖❖❖ TAKE-AWAY PRINCIPLES

1. Are there big differences between acoustic pianos and keyboard synthesizers?
Both acoustic pianos and weighted synthesizer keyboards are good options for the student. An acoustic piano or a weighted electronic keyboard will help the student build finger strength while practicing. An un-weighted synthesizer keyboard presses down easily like an organ and is not the best choice for the beginner, although it's better than no keyboard.

2. What is the best choice?
Ideally, I will always choose an acoustic piano over an electronic keyboard as I'm a discerning listener and hear the overtones an acoustic piano creates. This is my preference, but only if the acoustic piano is in good condition and will stay in tune.

3. What about tuning and maintenance?
Electronic keyboards (pianos) do not need extra tuning and are far more compact. If you are looking at a used acoustic piano, it is worth the extra money to hire a trusted piano tuner to check the piano out. A tuner is usually experienced in evaluating the basic mechanics of the piano and the shape of the hammers, action, and strings. An acoustic piano usually needs tuned twice a year with normal use.

4. Why start with piano and not another instrument?
Piano provides a great basic foundation of note learning, beginning music theory, coordination of hands and helps to develop the ear with basic harmony. Other instruments are also great to play, but once the student understands the basics of theory, it will be easier to add other instruments and even vocal training.

Katie and Rachel discuss electronic keyboards and what to look for in a private piano teacher.

CHAPTER THREE

Searching for a Piano and a Private Piano Teacher

Great teaching is not only about imparting content, but about fostering and nurturing the love for a subject. –Deborah Johnson

A whole month has passed and Katie is suddenly feeling healthier as she has just ordered her first non-fat cinnamon-dolce steamer. She now thinks of calling Rachel to thank her for the suggestion when her order is ready. She takes a delicious sip and as she starts walking out the door, she sees Rachel approaching.

"Is this the only place I see you, at Starbucks? That's scary!" Katie laughs as she turns around and walks back into the coffee shop with Rachel.

"Yes, it is scary. Generations from now, they'll wonder what the big deal was about Starbucks and think all we did was drink coffee."

Katie, laughing, "Well I'm glad to see you. This steamer is amazing."

"And healthy!"

"I'm feeling stronger already!" Katie continues, "And I just have to tell you, I have found some great used weighted electronic keyboards!"

"That didn't take too long!"

"It's been a month!"

"Already?"

"I know! But I have looked at so many. I'm leaning toward a Kawai."

"Kawai is a great keyboard, you can't go wrong there."

"But there were so many other great ones to choose from: Korg, Kurtzweil, Yamaha, Roland, and more! Am I even saying those names correctly?"

Rachel, "You're doing just fine!"

What to look for in a piano

"In fact, I almost bought a Roland the other day but the guy with the Kawai is so ready to deal and I like what the keyboard had to offer."

"Once you start looking for a used electronic keyboard, it's amazing how many are out there."

"I was actually surprised, some of them have hardly been used. But you were right to still check them out. They are all a little different."

"You mentioned all those other brands. What is it about the Kawai that you like so much?"

"The price is good. In fact, he's holding it until later today, so I'm going to jump on it. Also, it has a built-in speaker which is a major selling point for the amount of space I have. The whole keyboard fits against one of my walls. I don't need any extra cables or speakers besides the power cord, and of course some good earphones."

"I love earphones! They are great when kids are just learning."

"Yes, you're right. You just have to make sure they're practicing what they're supposed to practice. At least Shannon won't be playing violin or oboe at first!" Katie laughs, "I've heard some of the sounds that come out of those instruments when they're first learning!"

"Yes, listening to a beginning violin player sounds like a cat crying!"

And beginning oboe players?"

Together, "Like sick ducks!"

They both laugh as Katie continues, "Now I need to get serious about finding a teacher. Do you have any suggestions for me?"

What to look for in a teacher

"You're smart to ask, as a referral is usually the best way to go, but there are organizations to check out as well."

"Like the Music Teacher's Association?"

"You've done your homework! Yes, the M.T.A., or Music Teacher's Association is a great organization, but still always interview the teacher."

"How do I interview a piano teacher? I really have no idea what to look for. Maybe I should just get the name of your kids' teacher."

"You've interviewed people in your job, right? It's really not that much different. You basically want to meet the teacher and find out more about them."

"To see if you get good vibes?"

"Definitely. Get a feel for if Shannon would enjoy learning from them; you know her best. And let her meet the teacher too. Her opinion is important. You also should get a strong idea of what method the teacher uses and if they teach the basic chords and arpeggios."

"Is there a certain method to learning the chords, and what are 'arpeggios?'"

"As far as I know, there's no one best book for learning the chords, but a good teacher will incorporate them. Arpeggios are just rolled chords."

"Thanks for enlightening me. I'm feeling smarter already! So who do your kids take lessons from?"

"They have a great teacher they've been with a couple years, but unfortunately, she isn't taking any more students right now. She's been full with a waiting list for a long time."

"That's the type of teacher you want to get though, right?"

"Correct, but there are plenty of beginning piano teachers to be found. Basically you're looking for a teacher who can relate well to Shannon and is very excited about music. Most of the teachers should also hold performances. You did say that Shannon still loves to perform?"

"Anywhere with a stage is where she wants to be, but performances for beginning piano students?"

"When students have the goal of performing, they tend to practice more regularly and to concentrate on a deeper level. If they know a performance is coming, it helps them prepare more effectively."

"Good point. I never performed my piano pieces. I think I would have been petrified!"

"Maybe, but that's unfortunate you didn't have the opportunity and encouragement. If you had some good goals and a teacher who made it fun, it might have helped you enjoy piano more and even continue." When Rachel sees Katie pondering that last thought, she adds one more thing, "There are some college students who are good beginning teachers too, but the downside of a college student is that they usually move out of the area when they transfer or graduate."

"I want to make sure Shannon has a chance of sticking with her lessons. It would probably be good to find a teacher she can stay with for a good while."

"That's smart thinking. It may cost a bit more, but it will be worth it in the long run. Hey, I'd better get my order in. Let me know what you find."

Katie turns around to leave, "I will. Thanks so much Rachel!"

❖❖❖ TAKE-AWAY PRINCIPLES

1. What is the best brand and type of weighted electronic keyboard to buy?
When considering an electronic weighted keyboard, strongly consider one with a self-enclosed speaker, especially for an economic use of space. Many used products and brands are fine and will meet your needs. Focus on the basic qualities. Just as with purchasing a used car, the added bells and whistles aren't nearly as important as a basic good, reliable engine and well-rated safety features. With online ratings so prevalent, you can usually discern the better models and brands to pursue with the reviews and comments that are posted online.

2. What should you look for in a private teacher?
As far as finding a teacher goes, enthusiasm, along with a solid structure for learning goes a long way in keeping your student motivated. If a teacher truly loves music, that enthusiasm is usually contagious. If a student develops a deep love for music and for the piano, there is a greater chance they will practice more regularly and become more self-motivated to learn in the future, even on their own. Creating a "lifelong learner" is the ideal scenario.

3. What method should the teacher use?
Ask the teacher what method they use. (There are many good methods and the teacher may combine them.) Also ask if the teacher teaches chords and arpeggios. Chords and arpeggios are the building blocks in helping develop the ear and there is no reason to not start learning them right away; plus they're fun and provide immediate gratification. More about this will be covered in the next chapter.

Rachel and Katie discuss finding the right teacher and online piano programs.

CHAPTER FOUR

Hiring the Right Teacher

There are many options to finding a good beginning piano teacher today, even at local colleges. There are also online programs — although I believe the interaction between a live teacher and beginning student is the best choice. –Deborah Johnson

Even though she was now ordering steamers with the additional benefit of extra protein, Katie knew she needed to start getting in better physical shape. Her back was hurting and her energy was low. Her gym started offering a Pilates class and she soon was hooked. After starting to attend class regularly, her back was feeling better and the stretching exercises were helping to loosen the tight knots in her shoulders.

Katie was not flexible and couldn't even touch her toes, but she was thankful for the improvement she was making after only six weeks. She regularly attended on Tuesday and Thursday late afternoons, but she was fitting in a Wednesday session as she wanted to attend Shannon's piano lesson on Tuesday. As she situated her mat and started stretching, she started relaxing from her busy day.

Rachel had just joined Katie's gym and as a new gym member, Rachel wanted to try out a couple classes, including the Wednesday Pilates class. She gave a sigh of relief when she spotted Katie as she walked in with her rolled up mat.

"Katie! Hi!"

"Rachel! I didn't know you came to this gym!"

"I don't usually. I'm a brand new member and it's nice to see someone I know! Do you come here often?"

"Probably not often enough! Here, put your mat by mine. We have a couple minutes before class starts."

Rachel puts her mat down next to Katie then continues, "How are things going with the piano lessons?"

Referrals and professional organizations

"I just found Shannon a teacher!" Katie stretches out into a plank position, "You might know her. She's been teaching for a long time, but she isn't a part of the M.T.A."

"Not all of the great teachers are a part of the Music Teacher's Association, or even have a music degree for that matter."

Katie continues holding her plank position, "I did figure that one out!"

"I am so impressed with your plank! I don't think I could ever hold a plank like that!"

Katie laughs, "Of course you could!"

"We'll see." Rachel struggles to get into a plank position, but soon gives up as she crashes to the floor. "Some teachers have college degrees in different subjects than music, but they're still qualified piano teachers. How did you find Shannon's teacher?"

"A good friend at our church told me about her."

"That's great. Referrals really are the best."

"It actually took me three weeks to get an appointment to even see her, but she had an opening and I signed Shannon up right away. They really hit it off."

"You're smart to get her right in and it's very important for the teacher and student to hit it off. Congratulations! What sold you on the teacher besides the fact that Shannon likes her?"

What type of things should the private teacher teach?

Katie, finally getting out of her plank position, "When we arrived, one of her students was just ending his lesson and played some pieces for us. He played his piece with such feeling, and it wasn't just a normal classical composition that he was playing. Apparently this teacher also teaches the chords. I never learned the chords when I took piano. The piece he played was beautiful. It makes me want to pick up piano again just to play like that!"

"I'm so excited you found this teacher! Learning chords, right along with reading the music notes is the very best!"

"I always knew the guitar uses chords, but since I didn't learn the chords when I studied piano, I really didn't realize how important they are for piano as well. I'm definitely sold now, especially after hearing that student play!"

"Maybe you should learn the chords right alongside Shannon."

"Oh no, I was just kidding about taking up piano again! I was a failure at piano back in the day. I could never study piano again now!"

"If you just worked on your chords and basic five-note scales, you could be a success—I just know it! Maybe you should look into learning piano online. There are a lot of good programs out now."

"I don't really have the time. My schedule is so crammed."

"I know how hard it is hard to fit in one more thing; but I bet you'd love learning right along-side Shannon!"

Katie, "Actually, that does sound fun!"

Are online piano programs good for beginners?

"I just saw a great online piano program and you should check it out. I'll send you the link. The one I saw of only takes 15 minutes a day and looks like a great teacher teaches it! You can handle 15 minutes a day, can't you?" (Learn piano online with *Keys to the Keyboard*)[1]

"Maybe, but some of those online programs promise the moon!"

1. http://DJWorksMusic.com/learn-piano-online/

"They usually don't recommend an online program for children who are beginners unless it's just a supplement, but for you? I think you'd do well."

"Hmmm…O.K., I'll look into it."

"I'd hate for you to miss out this opportunity of learning with your daughter. Most of the online piano programs aren't that expensive. However, just like finding the right teacher has been important for Shannon, it's important to also find a great online piano teacher."

"I'm sure you're right. It's just deciding to start that's hard, and giving up the extra time to do it."

"Just like Pilates, but I'm giving it a try!"

"Hey, you'll be doing planks in no time at all! I think I see our teacher coming!"

"I did not plan on being in the front row. I meant to sneak in the back! I'm feeling sore, and embarrassed already!"

"You'll be fine! Just breathe…" Katie takes a big breath and whispers, "breathe…!"

❖❖❖ TAKE-AWAY PRINCIPLES

1. How do you find a good private piano teacher?
Start asking around as well as look at some professional teaching organizations. Also, don't discount a good college student to teach beginners. Just be prepared for change in a couple years if they move away from the area. A trusted referral for a teacher is absolutely the best. Katie found her teacher through a good friend at her church.

2. How should you interview a prospective teacher?
When meeting Shannon's prospective teacher, Katie was able to hear a current student play. She then knew her daughter would love playing the type of music this teacher taught. Shannon and the teacher also connected well, which is very important in the learning process, especially with private instruction.

3. What about learning piano online?
Katie became inspired to learn right alongside her daughter, which was a great idea. There are online piano courses available that don't take a lot of time or cost a great deal. Many of these programs add video to a structured program and are good options, especially for adult learners who maybe used to play and want to play again, now having more time. Do your homework and make sure the program covers what you want to learn, is taught by an experienced and qualified instructor and is easy to watch and listen to. The benefit of an online program is you can learn at your own pace, faster or slower, as long as you're consistent.

4. What about children learning online?
It is best for children to study with a live teacher, but for some, that is not always a possibility. Online instruction is better than no instruction, but for developing good technique, hand position and setting realistic goals for your child, a private teacher is the

best choice. Some online programs are very good as a supplement to other musical training, such as an additional resource for voice instruction. The addition of an online piano program focusing on the chords and other theory basics is optimal for learning the basics of the language of music and music theory.

Katie and Rachel discuss the basics a student should learn, as chords, five-note scales and good posture.

CHAPTER FIVE

Learning the Basics: Notes, Chords and Five-Note Scales

Learning the basic chords provides the fundamental structure of improvisation and of hearing harmony. –Deborah Johnson

Katie ended up signing up for an online piano program so she could learn right along with Shannon. After just a short time, she was hooked on learning the piano with the program and was excited to be learning right along with Shannon.[1]

Rachel is taking a much-needed break from her job, dropping by the local mall to window-shop. She checks her messages and notices a message from Katie. Instead of texting her right back, she decides to call. It only rings once.

Katie picks up, "Is this Rachel?"

"Yes! Hi Katie!"

"Thank you for calling me back so soon! I just sent you a text!"

---

1. Learn online with *Keys to the Keyboard*: http://DJWorksMusic.com/learn-piano-online/

"Your timing was great. I'm taking a few minutes to wind down at the mall and just checked my messages."

"I'm at the mall too! Wait... wait... are you in front of the candy store? I think I see you!"

"No way!" Rachel now sees Katie a couple stores down and laughs as they both walk toward each other. "Hi!"

"Hi! I called, mostly to thank you for all your great input on Shannon's piano lessons. Shannon just loves her teacher and I am thrilled!"

"Yay! That's much of the work right there—finding the right teacher! What is she working on?"

Learning the basic notes

"She's learning her note names of course."

"Of course—that's very important. How is she learning the notes?"

"This teacher is doing something I never did when I took lessons. She has Shannon sing the note names as she plays the notes of her songs."

"Playing one hand at a time?"

"You know so much more than I do about this."

"No, I've just gone through it with my kids. Singing the note names reinforces learning the notes, and it keeps Shannon singing at the same time!"

"I love it and so does she! It's not always easy for her, but it's keeping her even more interested."

"Singing the notes while she plays will also help her develop a stronger sense of pitch, especially when she plays notes in the bass clef."

"Pitch-yes, I'm learning how important pitch is and what it sounds like when they're off pitch!"

"We've all heard those singers on T.V. vocal competitions. What else is she learning?"

Learning the basic five-note scales

"The major chords. Of course, she's only learned one so far. The teacher is using the five-note scales to help her learn her chords."

"In what way?"

"Let's see if I can describe it correctly. Since there are five notes in the five-note scale, she first plays the entire five notes up and down. Then she just plays the bottom, middle and top note at the end all together—notes one, three and five—and they make a chord."

"You're doing great. My kids learned the same way—I was just checking!"

"It really makes sense. I'm actually learning so much too."

"As they learn the five-note scales, they learn the difference between whole and half steps."

"Intervals."

"You might not want to use that term at your job."

"Right! Have Eric and Catherine learned all their chords?"

Learning the basic chords

"Yes, all the major chords and they've gone on from there. Although Eric is starting to be more interested in girls and sports than piano right now."

"Don't worry, girls will fall for him when he sits down to play the piano! What other chords are there besides the major chords?"

"I wouldn't be concerned about those yet."

"Sounds good. I did sign up for an online piano program."

"Really? How is it going? Do you like it?"

"I just started and let's just say, I'm being challenged, but it's really fun! And you were right, it is great to learn right alongside Shannon."

"I wish I had more time right now for things I want to do."

"You're here—shopping is good! So the job's still stressful?"

"With a capital 'S.' This new position isn't all I expected it to be."

"I'm so sorry. Now I really appreciate you taking the time to call me back! Maybe you should start back into piano. You know...play it again!"[1]

"That could put me over the edge right now!"

"I don't know Rachel. I read somewhere that music can lower your stress level!"

"I do need something like that. I haven't even had time to get to Pilates class!"

"I noticed!"

"But I plan on coming back. Even the strong coffee isn't helping as much, but I'll make it. Tell me more about your online program."

"I'm just starting to play the chords and five note scales just like Shannon and I love the sound of them, that is when I can play them fast enough."

"How are the videos working? I'm assuming your program has videos?"

"The videos were easy to download and I can watch them over and over again, so that's good."

"So you can go at your own pace."

"Yes. It may end up taking me a little longer than six months as the program says, but that doesn't matter too much to me. In six months I'm supposed to be able to play some simple songs in different keys, using the basic chords."

---

1. http://DJWorksMusic.com/play-it-again/

"You might have played the piano longer if you learned the chords right along with the notes." Rachel continues, "I even know some classical pianists that can't get away from reading just the notes on the page."

"I think one of our church pianists is like that. She has to have the full music written out. Our worship guy doesn't use her because she can't read a chart with chords."

"That seems to be very common for some previous generations. It just wasn't as important to learn the chords on the piano; or new rhythms, for that matter. They basically focused on classical music and the notes. They would only learn the chords if they studied jazz or played the guitar."

"That's what I hear. I hope that if I keep learning the chords, I can also help Shannon as she learns. That is if she continues to listen to me!"

"I'm sure she will, at least until she gets a bit older. What is she now, about eight and a-half?" Katie nods and Rachel continues, "I am definitely having some listening issues with my kids right now. Especially after they spend a weekend with their father."

"But you're doing a great job. They seem very well adjusted. So you want to hear about the keyboard I found just for me?"

Having good posture

"You mean you bought another keyboard too?"

"Yes! It's only 61 keys instead of 88, but it was inexpensive, and it weighs about five pounds. I keep it in the hall closet.

Since my online program is demonstrated entirely on one of those smaller keyboards, I thought I'd get one for myself and it works great!"

"Now I'm really getting inspired, and jealous!"

"I can plug in my own pair of earphones and play away— and no one else can hear me, which is fortunate. But I should work a little more on my posture. I find myself concentrating so hard that my shoulders hurt!"

"It's hard to think about posture, as well as keeping your arms and shoulders relaxed while you're concentrating on something new. That may be why I'm feeling so tense in my new position at work. There has to be a connection between slumping and stress."

"You're not hunched over yet! So have you read any studies that say music can act as a stress-reliever? Just think—playing piano could help you give up those double shots of espresso!"

"No way! But I like thinking about playing piano again!"

Katie glances at the time on her phone, "Hey, I've really got to go but I'm so glad I got to see you!"

"You too. I'm going to take a few more minutes here."

"Buy some chocolate, you deserve it."

"That's the best idea I've heard all day!"

Katie, starting to walk away, "And don't forget to keep that posture up!"

"I'll work on it!"

❖❖❖ TAKE-AWAY PRINCIPLES

1. Why are learning the chords so important?
The chords help you get beyond the place of just reading notes. They provide the basic format for simple accompaniment patterns to play with melodies; plus they sound good! One more additional benefit is that chords help train the ear, which is extremely valuable in singing and basic musicianship.

2. What is a rhythm chart?
A rhythm chart can be in a number of formats. It can be in the form of a music chart with only the chords in each measure; it can have a melody line with the chords placed above the staff. (This is the format of most "Fake Books.") Learning the chords and the different types of chords provides the basics for playing many types of rhythm charts.

3. What are five-note scales and why are they important?
A beginning piano student, as Shannon is, can easily handle learning five-note scales as well as basic chords. The five-note scales will then be combined to make full octave scales as the student progresses. If the teacher or parent has the student also singing note names and matching the pitch of the five-note scales, it serves to help reinforce singing on pitch and further trains the musical ear.

4. Why is posture and relaxation important in playing the piano?
If your shoulders are tense, there is a good chance your arms and hands will also be tense. That stiffness can lead to physical problems, as carpal tunnel. Whenever you play a note, chord or phrase, you will use a certain amount of tension, but after playing a phrase or group of notes, totally relax the arm and hand. More about this will be covered in a later chapter.

Rachel informs Katie about more piano basics, including the arpeggios and use of the pedal.

CHAPTER SIX

Learning the Basics: Arpeggios and the Pedal

Playing arpeggios is fun, almost like playing the harp on the piano.
–Deborah Johnson

As Shannon continued her lessons in the following months, Katie also continued learning piano, working with her own online program. There were now days Shannon did not want to practice just what was on her lesson, but Katie was prepared. In order for Shannon to be successful and not quit as she had, she scheduled Shannon's practice time as a part of her school homework. She also did what she thought she'd never do; she provided small incentives for completing each piece or a certain number of days of practice in a row. It was working.

When her schedule allowed, Katie would either practice her own online piano program, or sit in to hear Shannon practice. Katie was starting to prepare for another important event in her life. She hadn't told too many people yet, as she wanted to make sure she was far enough along to lessen her chance of a miscarriage. She was now pregnant with her second child, expecting in just three months.

Katie thought she'd look more thoroughly into the studies and the claims of the *Mozart Effect*, which claims that by playing the music of Mozart, even while pregnant, your child could be smarter and more advanced. After reading some of the newest information, she realized it was based on a single example of a Mozart piece, and that many classical compositions could have the same calming effect as a piece by Mozart. She could understand the excitement about the study with so many parents, and many of her friends, anxious to increase their child's learning capacity, beginning in the womb. She did find some interesting information about spatial reasoning so she kept playing classical music when she could.

As Katie knew her life would change somewhat with a new baby, she wanted to keep encouraging Shannon and give her as much attention as she could. She also aimed to completely finish her online piano program by the time the new baby was here. Katie still attended her Pilates class and even though it had now been about five months since she had seen Rachel, when they both showed up at the same class, they picked up right where they had left off.

It is Saturday and Katie walks in with her mat. With her now growing belly, she doesn't want to commit to the front row, so she settles on a spot in the middle. As soon as she sits down, Rachel walks in and spots her.

"Katie!" She then looks at Katie's belly, "What happened to you?"

"Take a good guess!"

"Is Shannon still in piano?"

"Oh yes."

"And what about you?"

"I'm not quitting now!"

"I'm proud of you; and you're here in class too!"

"Yes, but getting a workout in is becoming a bit more difficult."

"What matters is that you're showing up!" Rachel puts her mat next to Katie, starts stretching, then gets into a plank position.

"I'm trying." Katie then sees Rachel in her plank position, "Look at you!"

"Yes, I'm learning, little by little. I've also started going to an early morning cycle class because of the great cardio workout; except today of course."

"I'd just die in a cycle class right now!"

"I feel the same way at the beginning of every class! But it's an amazing workout and a love-hate relationship. I hate going, but love when class is done!"

"Well, you look great! Shannon is having fun in her piano lessons, although I have to prod her to practice her actual lesson some days. But I'm happy she's singing right along with every one of her pieces."

"It probably keeps her interested. And it's really O.K. if she plays other songs too."

"Yes, I do know that. It's helped as she's learned many of her major chords now."

"She's only taken about six months, right?"

What are arpeggios and why play them?

"Yes, that's why I'm so thrilled. And I'm learning how to play the chords up and down the piano too."

"What about arpeggios?"

"Yes, even those. It's interesting to hear where the term came from—an Italian word that meant to play on the harp." Katie laughs, "I'm really slow with the arpeggios, but Shannon's learning them too. She's even using the pedal! It's cute—she can hardly reach the pedal, even with her toes!"

"That is so cute! I do know how much fun it is. Arpeggios are so good to get you comfortable using the whole keyboard."

"It's still a challenge, believe me! But they're very pretty. I do have some questions about the pedal."

Using the pedal correctly

"Sure. You're using an electronic keyboard, so you just have one type of pedal, correct?"

"Yes, we're using the pedal that came with the keyboard. But it looks like there are other types of pedals. I see little square ones and some that look like the ones that are attached on acoustic pianos. Is one better than the other?"

"They all work basically the same, but as long as your pedal works for your keyboard, you don't have to worry about the other types."

"The other types, meaning…"

"From what I know, there's a different polarity, positive and negative, on the electronic pedals, but many have a switch and you can use either one. I've never worried too much about that."

"As long as it works...."

"Right!"

"And the acoustic pianos have two or three pedals. Do I need to know about those when Shannon plays on an acoustic piano? Shannon's teacher says to use the pedal on the right for now."

"She's right of course, and you don't have to worry about the other pedals yet."

"That's what I figured. I'm hoping to finish my online piano program by the time this baby comes."

"Good for you. The beauty about those programs is that you can really go at your own pace."

"If you stick with them."

"Just like working out!"

Katie extends her arms in a stretch, "So right you are! I remember you saying you were going to sign up for one of those piano programs?"

"Actually, I did finally get around to it last month. I was able to go through it fairly quickly and easily."

"What? So fast! I wish I was at your level."

"I was actually surprised it came back so quickly—it ended up being an incredible refresher course for me and I'm glad I did it. When is your baby due?"

"Three months. I can hardly wait."

"I'm so happy for you. I know you wanted more children."

"Yes, we really did. It just didn't happen for awhile!"

"Getting back to Shannon, I'm so glad you are continuing her lessons. What type of pieces is she playing?"

"I guess they're still fairly simple, but they sound more involved to me as she plays all of them with both hands. She is learning so fast. Are your kids still taking lessons? They must be amazing by now."

"I won't let them quit, are you kidding?"

"What a super-mom you are!

"Superwoman, yeah that's me! Handling way too many things in my life!"[1] Rachel laughs and continues, "Work is plenty busy, but not quite as crazy since I've now settled into my new position."

"That's good. Gives you more time to play the piano again!"

---

1. *Superwoman* song here: http://DJWorksMusic.com/new-song-releases/

"I can't wait to dive into some new music. I have a couple of intermediate level titles I'd like to download soon."[1]

"I'm envious; you're actually able to play music you can download! I'm just playing these simple little nursery-rhyme songs."

"Never discount nursery-rhyme songs!"

"You're right. I sang many of them to Shannon when she was a baby!"

"And now you can play and sing them for this new little one! Many of those simple nursery-rhyme songs are at a great level for learning piano and your chords."

"I just feel like such a beginner, but I hope I can hear you play someday. Maybe I'll have you play something for this new baby!" The music starts and as the Pilates teacher starts speaking, both Rachel and Katie get into their first stretching position.

Rachel whispers, "That audience I wouldn't mind! Congratulations again!"

"Thanks Rachel!"

"Make sure you let me know when your new baby arrives!"

Whispering even softer as the teacher sternly glances over at the both of them, "I will!"

---

1. New intermediate level sheet music on SheetMusicPlus.com. Search *DJWorks Music* for Deborah's music

❖❖❖ TAKE-AWAY PRINCIPLES

1. Isn't note learning and reading music the most important things to learn at first?
Young learners are very capable of learning the notes, reading simple music and the chords at the same time. The fact that Shannon is learning her major chords right along with playing simple music with written notes on the page gives her a well-rounded music education right from the start. Reading music and playing with both hands together is also extremely good for hand-eye coordination.

2. What are the benefits of a parent learning basic piano skills right along with the student?
Some may think the student would be upset if the parent is also practicing some of the same things they are working on, but most of the time it helps the student see the discipline it takes to achieve a goal.[1] Katie is reaping the benefits of an online piano course by spending as long as she needs to get through each session, but is still modeling consistent practice for her daughter.

3. What is the best pedal technique?
If you are on an acoustic piano with a pedal, you should be able to comfortably put your foot on the pedal and lift up the front of your foot (toe) while keeping your heel on the floor. The same principle should work with an electronic synthesizer keyboard. If the pedal is not attached, you may want to attach it to the floor in some way. (Gaff tape looks like duct tape, but it's a professional grade that doesn't leave a residue on most surfaces.) Pedal technique is also covered in the online piano program *Keys to the Keyboard*.[2]

---

1. See more on goal setting here: http://DJWorksMusic.com/goal-setting/
2. http://DJWorksMusic.com/learn-piano-online/

4. Is an online piano course the best way to take a refresher course or is it better to study with a private instructor?

I will always first recommend a good private instructor, but for many, a good online course with a qualified teacher is perfect for getting back into the habit of playing the piano again. Many of the online courses go over basic skills that can be quickly reviewed at a varying pace. There are also many great sources for downloadable sheet music online and you can usually preview most of the selections on *YouTube* or with an MP3. Most importantly, when deciding on an online program, commit to consistent practice.

Shannon is learning her major chords, which is the beginning step of improvisation.

CHAPTER SEVEN

Learning the Basics: Improvisation

It's a fun skill that usually stays with you for life to take a simple melody line with chords and be able to play it with both hands.
–Deborah Johnson

Katie feels like she's getting larger by the day. Two and a half months have passed and she still has fairly good energy level, but her belly has grown larger at a quicker pace with this second child. Shannon is so excited about her new baby brother to be that Katie has to work harder to keep Shannon focused on her schoolwork as well as her piano practice.

Katie has kept up with her Pilates class, using the stretching as a therapeutic and relaxing exercise. She also wanted to keep working at her job until a couple weeks before the new baby was due, as both the money and the diversion have been nice.

Katie has now learned how to play simple chords and inversions with her left hand while playing a simple melody with her right hand. She is just learning her first song. Shannon is playing music that Katie is not playing, as Katie's online piano course is not taking her through a lot of note learning. However, she does not feel it is as important to her study and review all her notes as thoroughly as it is for Shannon. She will bring this subject up with Rachel the next time they talk. She hopes that Shannon will also be able to play simple chords and inversions with a melody line soon.

Katie stops by the store to pick up some newborn diapers. Her phone rings and she sees Rachel's picture pop up on her screen.

"Rachel! Hi!"

"How are you?"

"Big."

"I'll bet! I'll was just checking in on you."

"Yes, I'm due in a couple weeks now, so I'm just getting ready, you know, buying diapers and all that stuff."

"Things you haven't had to have around in awhile!"

"Yes—but it seems easier this time. I think I'm more relaxed. I'm also now playing *Twinkle, Twinkle Little Star* and hoping some of the classical music vibes rub off on this baby."

"Testing that *Mozart Effect*, huh?"

What is basic Improvisation?

"Not really, but it can't hurt and it's a piece I can handle!" Katie continues, "Being that I have you on the phone, can I ask you a question about piano improvisation? How soon should Shannon start improvising?"

"What is she working on now?"

"She's starting to play pieces with both hands together, but mainly with the music. She's also learning her chords, arpeggios and five-note scales."

"That sounds right. You really want her to know her notes thoroughly and play the actual written notes in both hands. It's like learning basic math for us."

"I thought that was important, but apparently I didn't learn math very well," Katie continues with a laugh, "because I can't play the written notes in both hands like she does!"

"Your goals are different than hers."

"That's true. If I had to go back and learn the math, I'd probably not continue."

"At Shannon's age, she can learn both the notes and basic improvisation and it provides a more solid foundation for her music education, as well as hand-eye coordination. For you, combining melodies and chords are fun and got you interested in playing again."

"I guess learning more notes will come later for me. For now, I think I've got plenty to handle."

"Yes you do, especially with a new baby coming. But now, as you know your basic chords, your next step will be to add some basic accompaniment patterns using your chords."

"Basic accompaniment patterns, or improvisation, right?" There is a moment of silence as Rachel nods, so Katie continues, "I think I'm just starting on that."

"I'm sure that's what you heard that student doing when you interviewed Shannon's teacher."

"Yes, the music just flowed."

"That is the beauty of learning the chords and using patterns for improvisation. They can really add so much to a piece of music. Eric and Catherine's teacher has them playing songs from a hymnbook."

Can a beginning student learn to improvise?

"A hymnbook? I haven't seen one of those in years."

"They still make them! The basic hymns are a great way to teach improvisation."

"How so? I've never heard of that."

"Most hymns are in different keys and use three basic chords, depending on the song and key."

"Like *Twinkle, Twinkle Little Star* uses three chords?"

"Same principle. You take the melody line, which usually consists of a couple notes played together, and then you add the basic chords in the left hand instead of the notes that are written. There are hundreds of songs and keys to choose from in a hymnbook."

"What a great idea."

"Apparently Elton John and other songwriters thought so too. If you listen to some of the songs written by Elton John, you will hear the basic three-chord pattern. It works."

"I guess, those three chords combined with a good melody line and good lyric can end up making you a lot of money!"

"If you're lucky!"

"So when can Shannon start playing in a hymnbook or some of the songs like the hymns?"

"That's up to her teacher, but I'm sure it won't be long. It sounds like Shannon's learning at a great pace."

"It seems so. She's still loving her lessons and is playing new things all the time, when she's not hugging my tummy!"

"How cute!"

"She's so excited about having a new baby brother!"

"Fun! A boy—I'm excited for you! Boys are great!"

"It will be different, I'm sure. I'm even more excited just looking at these little diapers! I'm almost up to the register, so I have to go, but thank you so much for your call Rachel."

"I can't wait! Keep me posted!"

"I'll try! Thanks!" Katie hangs up as the attendant starts scanning her items.

❖❖❖ TAKE-AWAY PRINCIPLES

1. What is improvisation in music?
Just like you may be familiar with a comic or actor making up lines on the fly, improvisation in music follows the same principle. At first, improvisation is more structured, with a basic formula of using chord patterns in varying keys.

2. How soon can a student learn to improvise?
A young student can learn the basics of improvisation right along with learning chords, but they should still have a solid foundation of notes, technique, hand position and finger strength. Basic improvisation begins with learning all the chords, major, minor, diminished and augmented.[1]

3. How important is it for a student to learn to improvise?
In my opinion, it is very important. Learning the basic chords and harmony, then adding chords, even in their simple form to a song, is a skill that brings enjoyment for a lifetime. Also, the development of the ear that occurs when learning the chords is transferrable to most other elements of music education, including learning differing instruments and singing harmony.

---

1. All are covered in *Keys to the Keyboard*: http://DJWorksMusic.com/learn-piano-online/

Relaxation of the shoulders, arms and hands, along with good posture and hand position are important, even for a beginning student.

CHAPTER EIGHT

Learning the Basics: Relaxation and Hand Position

Relaxation of the arms, shoulders and hands learned on a piano is a transferrable skill to other media, like computers and mobile devices.
–Deborah Johnson

Two weeks later, Katie delivered a healthy eight-pound baby boy named Ryan. She was happy that she had continued sitting with Shannon during her lessons and that she was on her way to finishing her own beginning online piano course. Every time she played the *Alphabet Song*, (also known as *Twinkle, Twinkle Little Star*, by Mozart) she kept thinking about the *Mozart Effect* and hoped her new baby would be positively influenced by her playing classical music.

A very nice card with a gift card arrived from Rachel, so she gave her friend a call.

Rachel answered, "Hello, is this Katie?"

"Yes, it is."

"Congratulations! I heard!"

"Thank you! And thank you so much for the gift card!"

"I figured you could use a couple things, now having a boy. How are you feeling?"

"Actually, great! I'm going to enjoy this time off!"

"I'm sure you deserve it!"

"Yes, I think I do deserve it!" Katie goes on, "Did I tell you we named the new baby Ryan?"

"No, you didn't. Great name."

"It means 'little king.' Shannon's good with it because she's always wanted to be a princess."

"I guess that works! Until she starts bossing him around, that is!" Katie laughs and Rachel continues, "How is she adjusting otherwise?"

"I've kept her in her regular schedule, including her piano lessons. I wanted to be as consistent as possible when the baby arrived. Shannon's teacher has started working more on hand position and relaxing the shoulders and arms. It almost seems like a bit much for her age."

Relaxing the hands, arms and shoulders

"Oh no, not at all. It's a good idea, no matter how young. I have some friends who took piano for years and have carpal tunnel."

"Just from playing the piano?"

"I'm sure it was probably from other things too, but playing the piano can definitely play a part."

"You can get it from doing anything repetitive, even computer work, and using the phone, right?"

"I think it can come from anything you do that creates a lot of tension."

"Like a lot of tension at work?" Rachel laughs and Katie continues, "Having the correct hand position has been especially hard for me."

"You probably had some bad habits to overcome."

"Yes, mainly from being on the computer so much. My fingers would just collapse or lay on the piano keys at first."

"How did you learn a more correct hand position?"

"I learned it not only from my program, but also from Shannon's teacher. If I make a fist with one hand and put my other hand over it, my fingers are naturally more rounded."

"That's a great way to learn to play on the pad of your fingers. It's particularly hard for those who have grown their nails long."

"It is. I ended up cutting all my nails. It's just easier."

"And they probably still look great."

How to work on relaxation while playing the piano

"I think so! Even though she's a beginner, Shannon's teacher also has her relax after every chord she plays and repeats with both hands."

"That's great she's learning that while she's so young. Eric and Catherine's teacher doesn't work on relaxation nearly enough and I have to think about it all the time since my teacher never taught me that way either."

"So it's not in your muscle memory."

"No it's not, but I'm working on it with some other finger exercises now."

"I'm sure that's helping. I'm glad my online program has insisted on good position and relaxation, even though it's been hard."

Rachel hears Ryan starting to whimper in the background. "Is that little Ryan I hear?"

"Yes, I think he's hungry."

"If that's as loud as he gets, you're pretty lucky."

"Oh, he definitely has some lungs, but I'd better go."

"Thanks for the call and I hope to see you soon. I can't wait to meet little Ryan!"

"I'll be around! Thanks again for the card!"

"You're very welcome!" Ryan's whimper is now escalating, so Rachel and Katie quickly end their conversation.

❖❖❖ TAKE-AWAY PRINCIPLES

1. How do you work on relaxing the arms, shoulders and hands?
If your shoulders are tense, there is a good chance your arms and hands will also be tense. You should be sitting a comfortable distance from the keyboard, shoulders down and relaxed, posture erect, arms level with elbows at about 60 degrees and fingers relaxed on the keys.

2. How short should your nails be?
You should be able to play on the pads of your fingers. (Make a fist with one hand and put the other hand over it, keeping the arms level. That will give you a good "rounded" position of the fingers that are placed over the fist with a level wrist.) If your nails are too long, they will get in the way. For beginners, it may be difficult to play on the pad of the finger without the finger "caving in." That is why piano finger exercises are important to develop good technique that will occur naturally when engrained in the muscle memory. If you practice the exercises correctly, you will build good technique that can be called upon for a lifetime because of the muscle memory you have developed.

3. Are there some recommended finger exercises that help you work on relaxation of the arms, shoulders and hands?
Besides relaxing after playing every chord to work relaxation in to the muscle memory, *Hanon* finger exercises are good for working on finger velocity strength and relaxation.[1] The exercises are very repetitive and good for building great habits. A good teacher will also work on using the exercises to work relaxation into the muscle memory.

---

1. *Hanon: Virtuoso Pianist in 60 Exercises*: http://www.amazon.com/ Virtuoso-Pianist-Exercises-Technique-Schirmers/dp/0793551218/ref= sr_1_1?ie=UTF8&qid=1431914800&sr=8-1&keywords=Hanon+Finger +Exercises

Performing doesn't need to be stressful!

CHAPTER NINE

Learning the Basics: Performance

Never discount the power of muscle memory in developing a skill.
–Deborah Johnson

Two months have passed since the baby came and Katie is back working part-time. She is now balancing work, a new baby and Shannon's school activities. Although it's busy, she is thankful that she likes her job and Ryan has been a very good baby. She's continued to nurse him, but is more relaxed on giving him formula now and then; different than when she had Shannon.

One thing is really bothering her. Shannon's first piano recital is coming up and as it is just weeks away, Katie is more nervous than she can ever remember being. Her stomach is tied up in knots and she finds herself being short with Shannon when she hears her playing through her songs too quickly, making more mistakes than needed.

Is performance important for beginners?

Before calling a counselor, Katie decides to call Rachel and talk to her about her growing feeling of doom. "Rachel?"

"Katie! How are you doing?"

"I'm back to work but I'm a mess! Shannon's recital is coming up."

"A mess? Why? How is she doing?"

"Shannon's thinks she's doing great. It's me that's not."

"What, you're performing too?"

"Oh no! But I'm more nervous than Shannon is, and I don't think she's ready."

"She's still practicing, right?"

"All the time. But sometime she gets her piece and sometimes she messes up. Did your kids go through this? And did you ever go through this?"

"Yes, and yes."

"So what do I do? Call the white coats?"

"Just make sure she's as prepared as she can be, then root her on! But I do understand and I feel your pain!"

"Her teacher recommended she slow her song down to make sure it's accurate, but she hardly does that. She plays like she's going to a fire!"

"She probably loves the way it sounds. Plus it's probably fun."

"It's not fun for me!"

"Having a newborn probably doesn't help."

"I have been a bit short with her. And it's been busy at work, but I'm managing. How do I deal with my nerves?"

How to cope with nervousness

"Just breathe."

"Breathe? I just went through that two months ago—I had a baby, remember?"

"Then you're in practice."

"This is not helping."

"Then what about drugs?"

"Seriously?"

"Really Katie, remember when you first told me how well Shannon was doing in all her school and class performances and how much she loved it?"

"Yes, but she was usually always performing with a group. This is different."

"There's a bigger chance of failing."

"Don't remind me! I don't want her to quit!"

"Don't worry, she won't quit! Is she nervous?"

"It doesn't seem like she is, but I'm really afraid she could be as she's playing her pieces so fast."

"Really, I think she'll do fine. As I said, you just need to breathe! It could have been you who had to perform."

"Oh wow, that's a good point. You really think she'll do fine?"

"I know so. Now don't get me wrong—she may make mistakes—but that's part of learning."

"It helps to talk about this. I am feeling a little better. I just don't know why I'm such a wreck."

"Probably hormones. Just envision Shannon performing and enjoying it. That may help you."

"Making it fun; that totally makes sense. It's just hard to do."

"I know. Wouldn't it be nice just to visualize everything going perfectly?" Rachel pauses, then continues, "Maybe we could visualize being in perfect shape."

"Oh yeah. I see a woman, slim and trim, moving gracefully through Pilates every move. Then I look in the mirror. There's a woman staring back at me with an extra fifteen pounds around the hips and butt. And graceful? Ha! I feel like the dancing rhino."

"Well at least you can still imagine that graceful woman!"

"But it only works so far in taking off those pounds!"

How to implement perfect practice and concentration

"Right you are. There is more to it than just thinking thin, but back to Shannon's recital. If Shannon combines perfect practice along with imagining herself performing, I just know she'll be a huge success."

"Perfect practice—yes. My online piano teacher also talked about perfect practice. There is something called 'myelin' that wraps around nerve fibers, similarly to rubber wrapping around copper wire and they make the signal stronger. With repeated deep and perfect practice done the right way, each new layer of myelin adds skill and speed."

"I think you read the same book I did! The thicker the myelin gets, the better it insulates. Then our movements and thoughts become quicker and more accurate. In fact, it's pretty amazing that without myelination, our spinal cord would have to be three yards in diameter! Perfect practice is really the key to improvement; playing each hand separately without mistakes, then combining the hands."

"Yes," Katie emphasizes the next word, "slowly without mistakes, the same way every time. Wow, we sound so smart!"

"We do, don't we? Perfect practice takes concentration and focus. I'm really sure Shannon will do fine, and you will too!"

"Yes, when she can focus and not look outside the window while she's supposed to be playing her piece."

"She can still be concentrating, but you know her better than I."

"I also know that thinking through a piece is an additional way to work on the piece, especially to memorize it. I've done that with poetry, but Shannon's a bit young to do that."

The importance of memorization

"Thinking through a piece, even away from the piano, works well especially for adult learners. Shannon's piece is memorized, correct?"

"Oh yes, her teacher insists on memorization for any performance."

"I'm sure she'll do well. Her performance goes to a higher level when she has her piece completely memorized. She and you will learn through this!" Rachel hears Katie taking a deep breath, then Rachel continues, "You'll make it, don't worry!"

"I knew you'd understand."

"I've been there, believe me! Hang in there, and let me know what happens!"

Katie breathes again with, "Okay! I'm breathing!" They both laugh as they hang up; then Katie takes a couple more deep breaths, hoping not to hyperventilate.

❖❖❖ TAKE-AWAY PRINCIPLES

1. Should you push a student, especially a beginning student, to perform?
I would encourage the student to perform, as performance provides the opportunity to set and reach goals. The teacher and the parent or caregiver can make this a very positive experience. Of course, there are instances where you can bypass the performance, since it's such an individual activity, but in most cases, an opportunity can be created to provide a positive experience for students. If performance doesn't occur in a group setting with a small audience (as in most recitals), encourage the student to perform for a small group of family or friends.

2. How do you deal with nervousness?
Nerves are a very real part of performance. The drama can escalate if fueled among students as well as parents and the teacher. There's a knack for taking the performance seriously, but also making it fun. Performance is a good opportunity to introduce specific goals with focused preparation, using concentration and perfect practice. Perfect practice is not just "playing the piece" but rehearsing a section or passage until it is correct with varying tempos and methods.

3. How do you develop perfect practice on the piano?
Here are some ideas: play each hand separately and slow down the *tempo* (speed), make sure you have good, relaxed hand position and your fingering is correct. Investing in a *metronome* (a device to keep time) will help you keep your tempo even while practicing. For years, I have related perfect practice to a well-crafted garment. When you purchase an article of clothing that is well crafted, it will hold together, whether or not you gain a few pounds. The stitching is solid, many times with double-sewn seams. A musical piece that is well learned and practiced will hold together like that well-sewn garment, even with the addition of nervousness or a change in environment.

4. Are there any other ways to practice?

For more advanced students, practicing a piece different ways, such as pretending to play one hand while playing the other also helps solidify memorization. (This method is called *pantomime*.) *Pantomime* is good for those students very reliant on their ear for memorization, as this method will develop the skill of actually visualizing the music and knowing where they are as they play the piece. By isolating the hands, they are able to discern any problem areas such as how well their memorization holds up in each hand and also any specific parts that they may have difficulty in playing.

Weekly Practice Chart

	M	T	W	Th	F	S/Su
Item Min.						
Item Min.						
Item Min.						
Item Min.						

A practice chart is great for keeping track of where you've been and where you're going. This one has places for items to practice, and minutes practiced.

CHAPTER TEN

Setting Goals and Deadlines

If you have well-defined goals in life, you've just spelled H-O-P-E.
–Deborah Johnson

It is early evening several months after the recital and Katie runs into the market for a couple healthy snacks and something easy to make for dinner. She doesn't linger long as she still has to make two stops to pick up both Ryan and Shannon. As she grabs a bag of chips, she sees Rachel checking out the barbecued chickens.

"Rachel! Picking up a chicken for dinner?"

"You guessed it!"

"Great idea. I think I'm going to do the same thing. They're so good."

"Yes, and easy! Hey, I haven't seen you since, but how did the recital go?"

"Thank you for remembering! I was so stressed!" Katie looks at the   chickens and puts one in her cart, "And I was so relieved when it was over!"

"Does that mean that Shannon did well?"

"I was actually surprised at how well she did! I was very proud of her; and I survived too!"

"I told you you'd make it!"

"I had my doubts! But Shannon ended up being very prepared and loved every minute of performing, especially with all the compliments she received."

"Sometimes our kids surprise us! Not all kids love to perform like that, but I still feel like it's a great experience for them. Most of the time, they pull though. So what's next?"

Setting new goals for the beginner

"Shannon's learning some new songs. She's very excited."

"That's great. After a performance is a good time to introduce new songs and material."

"I was afraid she'd lose momentum after the recital and the baby, but she's still excited."

"You know, a lot of it depends on you, as well as the teacher. You are so supportive of the teacher and I think it's also helped that you've learned piano right along with Shannon."

"I think so. We even compared practice charts."

"You had a practice chart? Oooh, can I see it?"

"Only a blank one!" Katie says with a smile, "But Shannon's teacher gave her a practice chart and we filled them out together. It took extra time for me to do it with her, but kept us both on track."

"Great accountability in action!"

"Yes, and I always do better if I have some sort of goal too."

"Most people are. The chart also probably helped you see how far you had come."

"Or didn't come, but good point!"

"You have come far! So what's next for you?"

"Surviving!"

"New babies will do that to you!"

"Shannon's teacher is starting her on some basic improvisation though, and I'm thrilled. I think it's been almost a year since she started now."

"Wow—a lot has happened in a year!"

"You're not kidding!"

"You may want to start downloading and reading through some simple sheet music yourself so you can learn and review all your notes."

"I'll definitely have to do some work in reviewing my notes before I do that. We'll see how much music I can really read. I haven't actually read the bass clef in years."

"You now know your basic chords, so just brushing up on the notes shouldn't take too long. I've really enjoyed playing some new pieces I found online."[1] Rachel loads her groceries on the register conveyor belt, "I'm sure reading the bass clef will come back."

"It's putting those hands together that's the challenge. But I do need to set some new goals and it's been fun to help Shannon add chords to some of her songs."

"Isn't it great that you can do that?"

"It really is! I'm actually surprised I can!" The checker starts adding up her Katie's groceries, "Those chickens look and smell like they just came from the oven. Yummy!"

"They are a guaranteed hit around my house! Love them!"

"I love it that I won't have to cook!" Katie swipes her card to pay, then picks up her bags to leave, "Stay in touch!"

"Don't worry! We really should actually plan to get together sometime!"

Katie, walking out, "Hey, what a novel idea!"

---

1. More new sheet music here: http://DJWorksMusic.com/buy-sheet-music/

❖❖❖ TAKE-AWAY PRINCIPLES

1. How important are goals?
Goals are very important for moving ahead, in music as well as in life. Music is a good place to start creating great habits in setting small goals, then larger goals.[1]

2. What types of goals should you set for the beginning student?
Even young children can start setting realistic goals, whether it's getting ready for a recital, finishing a school assignment, or learning major chords. I'm even in favor of creating small rewards that are appropriate for achievement.

3. How far along should a student be after a year?
It depends on the child. The student should at least know all their notes in both clefs, treble and bass, and basic five-note scales with major chords. They should also be playing simple pieces with both hands together.

4. How far along should a student be after two years?
Again, it depends on the child. The difficulty of the music should increase and occur at a good pace with a good piano repertoire book appropriate for the student. (The private teacher should choose this) A young beginning student should be successful with adding minor chords, basic arpeggios and very simple improvisation using the basic chords. The teacher should also add some sort of finger exercise book to work on velocity, finger strength, hand position and relaxation. (See *Hanon* exercises in previous chapter)

---

1. http://DJWorksMusic.com/goal-setting/

CHAPTER ELEVEN

Music and Stress

Together, melody, harmony and rhythm become a powerful and emotional tool. –Deborah Johnson

Snap! I felt my back lock up as I was bending down for one of my exercises at the gym. It was an exercise I call "shoveling" as you pick up a bar with a weight at the end, then lift it about waist high, move it to the left or right and put it down again. Weights, when used the correct way create a good kind of stress as certain muscles are designed to bear that weight. We get hurt when we use muscles that aren't meant to bear that weight.

I am happy to say that after a reasonable time of resting and stretching, I'm able to continue exercising again. I encountered the problem and got hurt because I wasn't using my gluteus maximus and hamstring muscles correctly. Putting weights on a bar is similar to adding stress. When used correctly and in the right amount, it can build muscle and strength. When used incorrectly, we can get hurt. All stress is not bad as it can push us to make positive changes. However, what we often find is that an increase of stress is a sign that something is wrong and needs changed in our life.

The calming and relaxing power of music

The calming and relaxing power of music is deep-rooted. It gives an exceptional connection to our feelings; consequently it can be a tremendously effective tool for stress management. Although musical preferences differ broadly amongst individuals, music in a classical style can bring a positive change in the physical and biological functions of our bodies.

Music has the unique power to touch the soul and deepest emotions of the individual. It can evoke the desire for repentance, it can stir tears and weeping for the loss of a loved one, it can bring sudden feelings of joy in the uniting of a new couple, and stir energy, excitement and motivation for pushing the body in exercise. We can see how music can even bring rest and relaxation by all the New Age[1] and other easy listening music that is produced every year. Much of this type of music is played in relaxing spas and venues around the world.

How music can affect the heart rate

The resting heart rate is about 60 bpm (beats per minute) for most people. With a slower song tempo, of between 60-80 bpm, the beat of the music influences and even calms the heart rate when a person relaxes and is in tune with listening to the music. Just as a cool bath succeeds in bringing down a fever, a slower pulse and rhythm works in slowing down the heart rate. Harvard Medical School reported that a nurse-led team found that heart patients confined to bed who listened to music for 30 minutes had lower blood pressure, slower heart rates, and less distress than those who didn't listen to music. Most of the music they listened to was identified as "restful or calm."[2]

---

1. Check out *Wayfarer's Journey* album by Deborah Johnson
2. www.health.harvard.edu/newsletter_article/using-music-to-tune-the-heart/

A tempo faster than 60 beats per minute seems to excite physiologically, but if the rhythm is even, the body can achieve a focused, alert state. The classical term for the tempo at 60 beats per minute is *Larghetto* or *Adagio*, which means slow. It is a ballad tempo and that's why much of the music you hear when having a massage is at this tempo. It tends to calm and relax. This type of "spa music" is usually repetitive with simple harmonies that tend to help the body, as well as the mind, relax.

Even while you wait for a facial or massage, you will notice this same type of "spa music" music being played. You start calming down and relaxing, no matter what your day was like, with the music, and sometimes the sound of running water, in the background. I look forward to arriving at a spa for this reason. I tend to run at such a quick pace that the calming style of the music and accompanying sounds start to help me relax immediately.

Playing this type of music with a calming effect in a spa setting may seem like a logical assumption, but it's also an interesting study to analyze the different styles of music between one storefront, compared to another. Is it easy, smooth jazz? Smooth jazz can have much the same effect as some "spa music" on relaxation, thus played frequently in restaurants. The goal is to create an atmosphere of relaxation and easy conversation to encourage the customer to order one more drink or appetizer.

When you walk into a contemporary clothing store, listen to the type of music that is piped in over the sound system. Both the style and volume are specifically aimed at the approximate age of the customer, hoping to create the type of familiarity or mood for a positive experience. At times, the customer may even be motivated to make a larger purchase.

Faster song tempos of 120-140 bpm are usually included in dance tunes. They are also great for running and working out because the faster beat influences a more rapid heart rate in the same way slower music encourages a calm heart rate. The music in my cycle class is at a faster tempo, with an electronic driving pulse. The aim is to push all participants to pedal quicker, harder and sweat profusely! I can attest that it definitely works.

How music can affect brain function

Researchers at Stanford University noted that music is something that almost *anybody* can access and makes it an easy stress reduction tool. "Listening to music seems to be able to change brain functioning to the same extent as medication, in many circumstances," said Gabe Turow, who was a visiting Department of Music scholar at Stanford University. Harold Russell, clinical psychologist, found that rhythmic stimuli that sped up brainwaves in subjects increased concentration in ways similar to ADD medications such as Ritalin and Adderall. The children tested made lasting gains in concentration and performance on IQ tests and had a *notable reduction in behavioral problems.* [1]

In my opinion, using music as an alternative to some medication and to enhance concentration is a great idea! In a society so dependent on popping pills and using substances to relax, music is a natural, simple and easy addition to the mix of remedies. Plus, there is no bodily harm to becoming addicted to music!

Using music as a diversion

Music also acts simultaneously as a diversion because it

1. Emily Saarman, "Symposium looks at therapeutic benefits of musical rhythm." Stanford News Service. http://web.stanford.edu/dept/news/pr/2006/pr-brainwave-053106.html

either absorbs our attention or provides enough background sound to enhance concentration on another subject. The field of music therapy is used very successfully with the potential to influence both psychologically and physiologically. Music therapy can be used in conjunction with biofeedback, guided imagery and other established techniques to help those with stress-related disorders. Stress related disorders include anything from anxiety to ADHD (Attention Deficit Hyperactivity Disorder), depression, panic and other syndromes.[1]

When the body and mind relaxes, there is a greater chance for any treatment becoming more effective. One of the reasons for this may be the relaxing effect of a calm tempo and melody. If the body remains in a tense and tight position, whether from nervousness, anxiety, fear or other reason, receptiveness to treatment is diminished.[2]

Using music in therapy

In the book *Musicophilia*, the famous neurologist Dr. Oliver Sacks tells the story of one of his stroke patients, a man named Samuel. Samuel was in his sixties and had developed aphasia, an inability to speak, after suffering a stroke. Despite extensive speech therapy he was unable to speak two years later. One day a music therapist at the hospital where Dr. Sacks worked noticed Samuel was humming. This intrigued her and she began meeting with him a few times a week to hum songs with him. Considered hopeless by speech therapists just two months before, the music therapist soon had Samuel singing "Ole Man River" and answering simple questions. [3]

1.http://www.nimh.nih.gov/health/publications/stress/index.shtml
2.Consider downloading *Wayfarer's Journey* at http://DJWorksMusic. com/wayfarers-journey/
3. Sacks, Dr. Oliver. *Musicophilia: Tales of Music and the Brain.* New York: Alfred A. Knopf, (2007) 214, 219-20.

I presently know a recent stroke victim who was not able to talk for some time. However, he can now sing a short musical phrase and is slowly learning to talk through therapy, using the same sounds and muscles he is using as he hums a tune. Just as a group of notes are connected together in a musical phrase,his family and therapists are working to connect groups of spoken words together in short sentences. He cannot start singing or talking in the middle of a musical phrase or sentence yet, as he needs to recite and connect them in the exact sequence he has learned, but there is hope that he will eventually improve enough to communicate more effectively.

It is interesting that the brain stem (back part of the brain) controls breathing, digestion, heart rate and other autonomic processes, as well as connecting the brain with the spinal cord and the rest of the body.[1] The brain stem is the part of the brain that is developed first for a baby in the womb. The cerebrum (or forebrain) makes up 75% of the brain by volume and 85% by weight, is largely reduced in size with Alzheimer's patients. There are still so many unknowns as to the cause and cure of Alzheimer's, but we do know that many patients respond to music.

I will never forget one of the last things I saw my father-in-law do was to sing a verse of *Joy to the World*. He had a wonderful career and was a brilliant man, but at the time, he had no idea who he was, who his family was or who his friends were from the effects of Alzheimer's. He died in his sleep within weeks of that singing episode. I find it interesting that at the beginning of life babies, even as their brain stem is developing in the womb, are capable of responding to music. Then, at the end of life, if a person is facing Alzheimer's or Dementia, even though the cerebrum may be highly damaged, an intact brain stem still allows one to respond to and even remember music.

1. http://www.human-memory.net/brain_parts.html

Music and speech may seem very different, but they both have *tempo, rhythm, intonation* (melody) and require the use of the same *phonatory* (vocal folds producing sounds through vibration) and *articulatory* (forming speech sounds) brain mechanisms. The experience of Dr. Sacks with Samuel opened the door to research in other areas, as autism, Tourette's syndrome, aphasic patients and others. As every human and situation is different, it's difficult to be certain of absolute effects, but the influence of music on the brain seems to be positive, thus the benefit of music therapy.

The idea that music has therapeutic qualities goes back centuries and provides a solid basis for the field of *Music Therapy.* Music Therapy is a rehabilitation process in which the therapist uses music with clients to improve or maintain their health. This is directly related to the fact that music has the power to reduce stress, thus decreasing depression, improving mood and reducing anxiety; all of which have the power to improve overall health.

Some say that music helps them calm down and sleep better. Those results will vary from person to person. I cannot listen to music or even work on a musical score before I sleep, as the melody of what I'm working on will continue to run through my mind all night long. However, that is not the case for everyone! There are many machines making white noise and nature sounds for the purpose of relaxation that some find very helpful.

Benefits of studying a musical instrument

Studying a musical instrument for recreational purposes can be great therapy because it takes a certain type of mental focus. The (mostly!) beautiful sounds created while learning to play chords on a piano or keyboard, or even on a guitar creates instant gratification as the notes are played together. I call note-learning the "math" of music. So many, especially in previous generations, have focused on the "math" instead of the expansion of expression in even simple improvisation by learning the chords and accompaniment patterns that are so pleasing to the ear.

Learning chords does not need to be difficult, especially with the many online piano programs available. (check out this six month *Keys to the Keyboard* program at link listed below)[1] If you are an adult learner, find a program where you can learn the chords and simple accompaniment patterns with a qualified teacher.

As stated by Barry Bittman, MD, CEO and medical director of Meadville Medical Center's Mind-Body Wellness Center in Meadville, PA, "Typical music-making is based on practice, performance, and mastery. In recreational music-making, our intention is to feel comfortable and nurtured in a creative experience with absolutely no pressure." Bittman also declares that, "One should think of music not as an end product but as a tool for health and well-being."[2] Concerning the use of music for recreational purposes, I agree with Dr. Bittman.

There are a number of ways people seek to relieve stress, such as owning an animal, traveling, cooking or other activity. Hopefully you will find that pursuing music, either by listening, recreationally playing an instrument, or both is a worthwhile option. I think you will find it extremely rewarding! It is something you can learn and enjoy many times over during your life. And it's just for you!

1. *Keys to the Keyboard* can be accomplished in 6,9,12 or 24 months depending on the individual. http://DJWorksMusic.com/learn-piano-online/
2. Kuchinskas, Susan. "How Making Music Reduces Stress." http://www.webmd.com/balance/stress-management/features/how-making-music-reduces-stress

❖❖❖ TAKE-AWAY PRINCIPLES

1. Can music really affect the heart rate?
With a slower song tempo of between 60-80 bpm, the beat of the music can influence and even calm the heart rate when a person relaxes and is in tune with listening to the music. (The resting heart rate is about 60 bpm.) Faster song tempos of 120-140 bpm are usually included in dance tunes and used in workout/exercise routines with much success, as the pulse and driving beat of the music helps push participants to cycle, run or work out harder and faster.

2. What effects does music have on brain function?
Some music has successfully changed brain function to the same extent as medication. There have been positive results for children with ADD, people with autism, Tourette's syndrome, aphasic patients and others.

3. Is studying a musical instrument really that beneficial and therapeutic?
Every case will be different, but the sound and even the feel of music touches the soul and emotions. Learning the basics doesn't have to be stressful or extremely difficult. For adults, learning the basic chords can be extremely enjoyable and fun. With the benefit of earphones, no one even needs to listen in! As you look around at the different ways music is used, whether in a shopping mall, spa or an exercise class, you can begin to feel the power of a melody, the excitement of a beat and the calming effect of a good harmony.

CHAPTER TWELVE

The Mozart Effect

As Mozart's music is rhythmically fairly simple, the patterns you learn in playing music by Mozart, or even by other classical period composers, can help develop mental skills for certain visual tasks.
–Deborah Johnson

Why Albert Einstein played Mozart

Albert Einstein, the brilliant 20th century scientist and inventor (1879-1955), used music as a tool to help him in his work. His second wife, Elsa, said, "As a little girl, I fell in love with Albert because he played Mozart so beautifully on the violin." She continues, "Music helps him when he is thinking about his theories. He goes to his study, comes back, strikes a few chords on the piano, jots something down, returns to his study." His older son, Hans Albert, said, "Whenever he felt that he had come to the end of the road or into a difficult situation in his work, he would take refuge in music."[1]

---

1. http://www.pha.jhu.edu/einstein/stuff/einstein&music.pdf

What is the Mozart Effect?

There has been much talk and varying opinions about what is called the *Mozart Effect* in the past decade. The *Mozart Effect* is defined as: "...listening to Mozart's music may induce a short-term improvement on the performance of certain kinds of mental tasks known as 'spatial-temporal reasoning.'"[1]

As far back as 1977, a study was conducted on preschool children to determine ability for spatial-temporal reasoning, with and without keyboard lessons. Four groups of children were tested, then re-tested after six to eight months, one group receiving keyboard lessons. Out of the four groups, none of the groups showed significant growth except for the group with piano keyboard lessons, their score rising from ten to fourteen out of fifteen possible.

The study also questioned if the effects were long-term and discovered no significant difference in the children who were tested immediately after the lesson or one day or more after their last piano keyboard lesson. When the testing results last at least one day, the outcome is determined to be long-term. This is important because the results suggest that piano keyboard lessons for any reasonable length of time can have long-term effects on spatial reasoning.

Mozart and spatial reasoning

Spatial reasoning is defined as the ability to visualize with the mind's eye. (think "picture smart") Howard Gardner, an American developmental psychologist, says it is a human capacity

1. Pryse-Phillips, William. *Companion to Clinical Neurology.* New York: Oxford University Press (2003) 611, defines the term as "Slight and transient improvement of spatial reasoning skills, detected in normal subjects as a result of exposure to the music of Mozart, specifically his sonata for two pianos." (K448)

that provides the ability or mental skill to solve spatial problems of navigation, visualization of objects from different angles and space, recognition of faces and scenes or to notice fine details. In other words, spatial reasoning is the ability to think in three dimensions.[1] 3D technology is becoming more and more popular in media and music as it helps stimulate reality in the imagination. Spatial reasoning can help stimulate that 3D reality in the mind.

Why the music of Mozart?

The term *Mozart Effect* goes back to 1991 when Dr. Alfred A. Tomatis, a French researcher, described for the first time the concept of the *Mozart Effect* in his book, *Pourquoi Mozart? (Why Mozart?)*[2] He proposed alternate medicine for resolving such conditions as autism, dyslexia and other syndromes. Dr. Tomatis employed music in the course of therapy sessions and claimed that music by Mozart really assisted in stimulating the healing and curing of patients.[3]

Governor Zell Miller of Georgia was fascinated by the outcomes of the study by Tomatis. The legislature approved a bill that every new mother in the state should be given a free CD or musical tape of Mozart (remember cassette tapes?) and for this, $105,000 was allocated for "Mozart for the Masses."[4]

Soon, the states of Tennessee and Florida followed suit. In 2000, the state of Florida ensured that classical music was played in day care centers. A community college in New York formed a *Mozart Effect* study room.[5] It was a good day for musicians as

1. http://faculty.washington.edu/demorest/rauscher.pdf
2. http://en.wikipedia.org/wiki/Spatial_intelligence_(psychology)
3. Tomatis, Alfred. *Pourquoi Mozart?*:Essai (French Edition) New York: Hachette (1991) http://www.amazon.com/Pourquoi-Mozart-Essai-French-Edition/dp/2876451077
4. http://www.cs.rutgers.edu/~biglars/Mozart.html
5.http://www.nytimes.com/1998/01/15/us/georgia-s-governor-seeks-musical-start-for-babies.html

many hopped on board to be a part of creating music for those bills.

The commercial power of the Mozart Effect

Since then, the *Mozart Effect* has been widely debated, but mostly because there have been many claims stating that merely by listening to the music of Mozart, kids can raise their IQ. Don Campbell, a classical musician and former music critic, was the first to recognize the research's commercial potential. Campbell expanded the definition of the *Mozart Effect* to include all music's influence on intelligence, health, emotions and creativity.

In 1996, Campbell trademarked The *Mozart Effect*[1] and ran with the brand. Campbell has authored eighteen books, a series of spoken tapes, and sixteen albums incorporating Mozart's music. One of his recordings, which features *Don Giovanni* for the developing fetus, sold over two million copies.

Playing Mozart and playing football

In 2007, Eric Mangini, as coach of the *New York Jets*, added Mozart to the music playlist to entertain the fans showing up every day to watch practice. He was working to get every advantage he could get, especially during the low-intensity drills when the team split up into individual units. With these low-intensity drills, the coaches were stressing mental work over physical.[2] Apparently, Mangini felt that listening to Mozart would increase the player's ability to concentrate while executing their drills.

My husband found the *New York Jets* information interesting. As a former professional minor-league baseball

1. Campbell, Don. *The Mozart Effect.* New York: Avon Books, 1997.
2. http://www.nydailynews.com/sports/football/jets/mangini-players-tuned-article-1.266527

player, he had never heard of a professional sports team playing Mozart during practice. I'm not sure how his baseball team, the *Indians*, would have responded. The opinion of the coach would greatly determine whether the music by Mozart would be played, based on whether or not he thought there would be any benefit for the players by playing the music.

Mozart lived and composed in the Classical era, which featured clarity, balance and transparency. Music from the Classical period was much lighter in style than music in the earlier Baroque era. From this we see that music by Mozart, as it's from the Classical period, is usually easy to listen to and calming to the ear. As our emotions are usually aroused when something interesting occurs, the clarity, order and simplicity of Mozart's music would seem to keep feelings steady and balanced.

While the commercial success of products associated with the *Mozart Effect* still seem to do well, it is a theory somewhat flawed in its scope. The flaws are mainly due to many unsubstantiated claims that merely by listening to Mozart, kids can raise their IQ. However, the German Ministry of Education and Research did come to the defense of the *Mozart Effect's* usefulness in a few key areas. First, there was a positive effect on IQ for those who undergo musical training. This is a logical assumption as skills developed in becoming a proficient musician may aid in acquiring knowledge and understanding. (see the discussion of myelin and muscle memory in chapter nine)

The German Ministry of Education also reviewed a paper written in 1998 that claimed that listening to Mozart reduced seizure rates for people with epilepsy. In this study, twenty-three of the twenty-nine patients experienced significant decreases in epileptiform activity, which are the brain waveforms recorded during a seizure, even from patients in comas. [1]

1. http://www.cs.rutgers.edu/~biglars/Mozart.html

An experiment by John Hughes, Director of the Epilepsy Clinic at the University of Illinois at Chicago, had considerable clinical potential. John played the *Mozart Sonata* (K.448) to epileptic patients who had many, usually repetitive focused discharges either when awake or in a coma. In twenty-nine out of thirty-six cases, there were statistically significant decreases in the epileptic activity as measured in surface brain waves. This was not attributed to relaxation, but to the clear effects of playing of the music of Mozart.[1]

Should you play Mozart for your babies in the womb?

Should young mothers, or mothers-to-be play music by Mozart for their children, even while still in the womb? In my opinion, it doesn't hurt! According to *Amplifon*, an organization dedicated to hearing with over sixty years experience and more than 5,700 specialist centers in over twenty countries, hearing organs start forming when a baby is just three weeks old in the womb, starting at the inner ear and slowly building up to the ear canal.

It is thought that the auditory system becomes functional at around twenty-five weeks. Hearing development also improves as the brain becomes more complex, detecting different moods and emotional responses to speech and music at around thirty-six weeks old.

Amplifon has conducted their studies by inserting a small hydrophone into the uterus of a pregnant woman, then testing the heartbeat under different conditions. They found that tone is particularly important with unborn babies responding to changes in pitch when music is playing.[2]

1. Shaw, Gordon L. *Keeping Mozart in Mind*, 2nd Edition. Amsterdam: Academic Press, Elsevier. (2003) 38-40
2. http://www.amplifon.co.uk/resources/how-babies-develop-hearing/

I agree with some of the skeptics that say we are not making our kids smarter merely by listening to music by Mozart, although the evidence does suggest that listening can further develop spatial reasoning. I tend to naturally agree with that statement because of the focus, order and calmness that occurs by listening to music by Mozart, or even to music by other composers similar to Mozart.

Does playing classical music really make your kids smarter?

Going a step further, if you choose to study and play music by Mozart, I believe there is an additional advantage. As Mozart's music is rhythmically fairly simple, the patterns you learn in playing music by Mozart, or even by other classical period composers such as Clementi and Vivaldi, can help develop mental skills for putting together certain tasks. Visualizing a musical phrase and developing a deeper understanding of form and structure are transferrable concepts and skills. Those skills of visualization and structure can be applied, whether in studying for exams, writing proposals or organizing a business. The reason for this, as previously discussed, is the music of the Classical period is defined as music with order and consistent form; thus the sequence and orderliness of the style can be applied to other areas.

In a society and world that is full of constant change, interruptions and chaos, music with order and consistency is a welcome respite from the confusion. For me, even playing the music of Mozart on the piano provides a relaxing and calming effect, as it is not technically difficult for me or harmonically dense. This may also be why the music has a calming and soothing effect on the listener. I love music and it is my hope that you have caught a bit of my love, conviction and excitement for the spreading of that love of music by reading this book.

My husband studied piano for eight years, taking private lessons all the way through primary and secondary grades. His one regret was not being introduced to chords. He only learned about the chords when picking up a guitar. Even though he will sit down and play once in awhile, I believe he could have enjoyed playing much more if he had also learned the basics of improvisation with his chords.

As we have raised three sons, they all took private piano lessons, at least for a while. They did each go on to study other instruments. I am happy to say that they have each developed an appreciation and ear for music and hope they will pass that legacy along to their children. Of course, at this stage, it is totally their decision, but they will soon be at the crossroad where they can determine whether they wish to impart the love of music to their own children.

Even though we've looked at the benefits of the music of Mozart, of music in general and of keyboard lessons, it all comes down to having a love of music. Actually, in my house as I've been married now for a number of years to a former professional baseball player, it doesn't just come down to the love of music. In my home, no matter what the conversation, it all comes back to baseball. Here's hoping that you hit it out of the park!

❖❖❖ TAKE-AWAY PRINCIPLES

1. What is spatial reasoning and how is it related to the *Mozart Effect*?
In today's language, spatial reasoning is the ability to see and imagine in 3D. As far back as 1977, the group of children that were tested before and after keyboard lessons showed significant growth in spatial reasoning. The *Mozart Effect* was directly linked to this study with further studies on playing the music of Mozart.

2. Why was the music of Mozart played during football practices?
In 2007, Eric Mangini, coach of the *New York Jets*, added Mozart to the music playlist as he felt that listening to the music of Mozart would increase the players ability to concentrate while executing their drills. Although there may be teams presently doing this, I've not heard of any.

3. Does playing the music of Mozart help babies while still in the womb?
We do know that unborn babies, according to the research of *Amplifon*, can hear tones in the womb. In fact hearing organs start developing at just three weeks old and are fully functional at twenty-five weeks. There is no documented study that says kids turn out smarter merely by listening to the music of Mozart, or even other composers, while still in the womb. However, I feel there could be positive growth in spatial reasoning and influence on heart rate. I am definitely in favor of adding listening to good music at any stage of development, whether for unborn babies, young children, or adults.

QUOTABLE MUSICIAN
QUOTES

Did I want to go to a music lesson? No, I wanted to play football on the street. As a parent, you try to guide your kids in a certain direction as painlessly as possible. You don't want them to equate every pursuit that is not pure frivolity with pain. -Wynton Marsalis[1]

One good thing about music is that when it hits you, you feel no pain. -Bob Marley [2]

The piano ain't got no wrong notes. -Thelonious Monk[3]

Everybody told me this 'girl on the piano' thing was never going to work. -Tori Amos[4]

One of my biggest thrills for me is sitting down with a guitar or a piano and just out of nowhere trying to make a song happen. -Sir James Paul McCartney[5]

---

1. Wynton Marsalis, Director of Jazz at Lincoln Center in New York City, U.S. Nine-time Grammy Award winning composer and trumpet player. (Thompson, Jane. "Interview with Wynton Marsalis." National Post, April 24, 1999, vol. 1, no. 153, 3)
2. Bob Marley, Jamaican reggae singer, songwriter, musician and Grammy Lifetime Achievement Award winner (1945-1981)
3. Theolonius Monk, jazz pianist and composer. (1917-1982) Known for his unique improvisational style and made numerous contributions to the standard jazz repertoire.
4. Tori Amos, American pianist, singer and songwriter nominated eight times for a Grammy Award.
5. Sir James Paul McCartney (Paul McCartney), English singer-songwriter, multi-instrumentalist and composer. Former member of the Beatles and has sold over 100 million albums and 100 million singles. Twenty-one time Grammy Award winner.

Sometimes I can only groan, and suffer, and pour out my despair at the piano! -Frederic Chopin[1]

Prayer is when you talk to God. Meditation is when you're listening. Playing the piano allows you to do both at the same time. -Kelsey Grammer [2]

If I'm going to Hell, I'm going there playing the piano. -Jerry Lee Lewis [3]

Without a piano I don't know how to stand, don't know what to do with my hands. -Norah Jones[4]

I was a strange, loud little kid who could sit at the piano and kill a Beethoven piece. -Lady Gaga[5]

If I hadn't been President of the United States, I probably would have ended up a piano player in a bawdy house. -Harry S. Truman[6]

---

1. Frederic Chopin, (1810-1849), Polish composer and virtuoso pianist of the Romantic Era, writing mostly for solo piano.
2 Alan Kelsey Grammer, American actor, voice actor, comedian. Winner of five Emmy Awards and three Golden Globe Awards. Known for Dr. Frasier Crane on *Cheers* and a voice artist on *The Simpsons*.
3. Jerry Lee Lewis, American singer-songwriter, musician and pianist often viewed as "rock & roll's first great wild man." Winner of several Grammy Awards as well as the Lifetime Achievement Award.
4. Norah Jones, American singer-songwriter, musician and actress. Winner of nine Grammy Awards, selling more than 50 million albums worldwide.
5. Lady Gaga (Stefani Joanne Angelina Germanotta), American singer, songwriter and actress. Six time Grammy Award winner and one of the best-selling musicians of all time.
6. Harry S. Truman (1884-1972), 33rd President of the United States (1945-53). He got up every day at five A.M. to practice the piano, which he studied twice a week until he was fifteen.

After I learned the piano, I went on to learn percussion, the tuba, B-flat baritone, French horn, trombone, trumpet, most of the instruments in the orchestra. -Quincy Jones[1]

The piano is a universal instrument. If you start there, learn your theory and how to read, you can go on to any other instrument. -Eddie Van Halen[2]

I went to college on a classical piano scholarship. My grandmother made me practice one full hour a day. Every day. Man. I thought all she wanted was for me not to have any fun. Next thing you know, you have a career in music. Now, not everybody's going to go on and be Mozart or Michael Jackson. But music makes you smarter. -Jamie Foxx[3]

---

1. Quincy Jones, American record producer, conductor, arranger, composer, musician and producer with seventy-nine Grammy Award nominations, and twenty-seven Grammy Awards, including the Grammy Legend Award.
2. Eddie Van Halen, Dutch-born American musician, songwriter and producer. Best known as the lead guitarist, keyboardist and co-founder of hard rock band *Van Halen*. He has been voted as number one of "The 100 Greatest Guitarists of All Time."
3. Jamie Foxx (Eric Marlon Bishop), American actor, singer, comedian, writer, producer. Winner of both an Academy Award and Grammy Award. Began playing the piano when he was five years old and as a teenager was the New Hope Baptist Church's part-time pianist and choir leader.

Definitions of Musical Terms

Dynamics
Loudness and softness of the music.

Ear Training
Notes, intervals and chords played or performed without written music.

Five Note Scale
A pattern of five notes moving in whole steps up and down, except for one half step between notes three and four.

Half-Step
The smallest distance between two pitches in Western music.

Harmony
The sound when two or more tones are combined or played together. Harmony consists of *dissonance* (clashing) or *consonance* (pleasing).

Improvising
Creating and composing while playing. Basic improvisation begins with the chords.

Interval
The distance between two notes or pitches.

Jazz
A popular style of music with roots in shouts, calls, spirituals and gospel songs, developed in early twentieth-century America.

Major Scale
A pattern of eight notes moving in whole steps up and down, except for two half steps between notes three and four and seven and eight.

Melody
The main tune of a song.

Metronome
A mechanical or electric device that makes repeated clicking sounds at an adjustable pace used by musicians and music students to help keep time in practicing.

Music Therapy
A rehabilitation process in which the therapist uses music with clients to improve or maintain their health.

Octave
The distance of pitch eight notes apart, such as C-C, D-D, E-E.

Pantomime
In piano music, pretending to play one hand while playing the other. (One hand is completely silent while still fingering the notes.)

Pitch
The high and low of a sound.

Range
The highs and lows of a piece of music.

Rhythm
The duration of the notes and sounds of the music. It can also include the silences.

Scale
The pattern of notes, ascending or descending in half or whole steps.

Spatial Reasoning
The ability to think in three dimensions.

Tempo
The rate of speed of a piece of music.

Whole Step
The distance between two notes equaling two half steps.

About Deborah Johnson

Deborah Johnson is the president and founder of *DJWorks Music* and *Worthy Acts*. She is not only a headliner artist, but also speaker, author, composer and educator with a Master of Arts degree in composition and arranging. Deborah began taking piano lessons at the age of nine and quickly progressed, as her teacher realized she could play by ear and improvise easily. She started combining playing the piano with singing quite early on, her skill propelling her to be one of the top women vocalists/pianists in the world.

Deborah started studying classical piano in high school with Joanna Hodges, the first woman concert pianist to perform in Communist Russia. Joanna not only taught her good technique, expanding her repertoire for performance, but the discipline to compete in major concerto and other classical competitions. She began her college education with emphasis in both piano/ vocal performance and education, and ended up achieving both a secondary teaching degree, then a masters degree.

With over two dozen albums, three full-length original musicals with national distribution and several books under her belt, Deborah is a part of a unique group of women entertainers and composers in the world. She has also recorded and performed on many large stages with Wayland Pickard, part of the piano duo, *Double Grandé*.

In the past years, she has been up for multiple Grammy Awards for her original songs, arrangements and albums. In 2014, she entered the speaker world by developing a new book with a motivational keynote entitled, "Getting Your Life Unstuck."

Deborah is also a long-distance runner; she runs her businesses, her home and keeps up with three amazing sons and a husband.

Websites: DJWorksMusic.com; DoubleGrandePianos.com; WorthyActs.com

Made in the USA
Charleston, SC
08 November 2015